NORTH AMERICAN FIELD GUIDES

CONIFERS

Laura K. Murray

Field Guides

An Imprint of Abdo Reference | abdobooks.com

CONTENTS

WHAT ARE CONIFERS?

Conifers are woody plants that produce their seeds in cones rather than flowers. Conifers may grow as trees of various sizes. They may also grow as shrubs with several stems or trunks. Other conifers grow low and spread across the ground.

Nearly all conifers have either scale-like or needle-like leaves. Scale-like leaves are small and flat. They often overlap with one another. Needle-like leaves are long, thin, and pointed. Most conifers are evergreen, meaning they keep their leaves all year long instead of dropping them each year. However, there are a small number of deciduous conifers. These species drop all or most of their leaves in fall.

Cones of conifer species are different sizes, shapes, colors, and textures. Male cones produce pollen. Female cones produce seeds. Many conifers have both male and female cones on a single tree. Some conifers need heat to melt the resin that seals their seed cones shut. Most often the heat comes from a wildfire. But other conditions can also cause cones to open, such as hot sun or dryness. Once the cone opens, the seeds inside can drop to the ground.

THE IMPORTANCE OF CONIFERS

Conifers are an important part of the world's forests. They provide homes and food for wildlife. Humans use these trees' wood for lumber, fuel, paper materials, and more. People also use the resin of conifer trees for oils and medicines.

Today many conifers face threats from both nature and humans. The trees are at risk from pests and disease. Other threats include wildfires and climate change. Habitat loss and deforestation have destroyed some conifer populations, leading to certain conifers being classified as endangered species.

CONIFER IDENTIFICATION

There are more than 600 species of conifers, with much variety within this group. Some conifers grow quickly, while others grow slowly. These hardy plants can survive in cold and snowy conditions and in milder climates. Some survive in rocky, dry soil. Others flourish on riverbanks or in swamps.

People can use several traits to identify conifer species. For example, observers can estimate the height of a tree and compare it with the average height of a species. The color, shape, and arrangement of leaves can also indicate a tree's species. Cones differ between species and are often used as tools for identification. Female seed cones are especially distinctive. Looking at the ranges and habitats of different species can also help people identify trees. However, conifers may grow outside of their native ranges as part of home and business landscaping.

HOW TO USE THIS BOOK

Tab shows the conifer category.

REDWOOD FAMILY

COAST REDWOOD

(SEQUOIA SEMPERVIRENS)

...dwood grows along the Pacific Coast. It is also ...od. It is the tallest tree on Earth. ...n) each year. The California ...longest-lived trees. It can live for ...e base of a tall tree can be more than 20 feet (6 m) ... The tree's rough, reddish-brown bark may be up to two feet (0.6 m) thick. Coast redwoods can sprout from stumps and roots. *Sequoia*, the name of this genus, was given in honor of the Cherokee chief Sequoyah.

The conifer's common name appears here.

HOW TO SPOT

Height: 60 to 380 feet (18 to 116 m)

Leaves: Needle-like; bright or dark green with two white lines on undersides; 0.5 to 1 inch (1.3 to 2.5 cm) long

Seed Cones: Egg ...haped; brown; 0.5 to 1 inch (1.3 to 2.5 cm) long

North American Range: Pacific Coast of southwestern Oregon to central California

Habitat: Moist and foggy coastal plains and slopes

How to Spot **boxes give information about the conifer's size, leaves, seeds, range, and habitat.**

...ETTING WATER FROM FOG

Redwoods need up to 160 gallons (606 L) of water each day. During the dry summer, redwoods rely on fog for water. T...ey may get up to 40 percent of their water from fog eac... year. But climate change is a threat. As global tempera... ...rise, there is less coastal fog. It is harder for tree...

Sidebars provide additional information about the topic.

GIANT SEQUOIA

SEQUOIADENDRON GIGANTEUM

The conifer's scientific name appears here.

The giant sequoia's scientific name means "gigantic." It is the largest tree on Earth by volume. Although some trees grow taller, the giant sequoia is thicker. Its trunk can be up to about 30 feet (9 m) across and more than 94 feet (29 m) around. The tree loses its lower branches as it ages. The reddish-brown bark is spongy. The seed cones may stay closed for 20 years before opening with fire or other heat. Each cone produces about 200 seeds. The giant sequoia is an endangered species.

This paragraph gives information about the conifer.

HOW TO S

Height: 250 t (76 to 84 m) or

Leaves: Scale-like; bluish green; 0.1 to 0.2 inches (0.2 to 0.5 cm) long

Seed Cones: Egg shaped or oval; reddish brown; 2 to 3.5 inches (5 to 9 cm) long

North American Range: Sierra Nevada in California

Habitat: Cool, moist mountainous areas

FUN FACT

Giant sequoia trees often live to be more than 3,000 years old.

Seed cone

Images show the conifer.

Fun Facts give interesting information about conifers.

ARIZONA CYPRESS

(HESPEROCYPARIS ARIZONICA)

The Arizona cypress is a common tree throughout the southwestern United States. It usually grows tall with a wide, cone-like shape. In some places, the Arizona cypress grows shorter and shrub-like. Its leaves are small, soft, and scale-like. The leaves grow on thick branches. They may look gray or silver. They give off a fragrant scent when crushed. The gray outer bark is rough and scaly, and it peels away to show reddish inner bark. Seed cones open after their branch dies from age or wildfire.

HOW TO SPOT

Height: 40 to 75 feet (12 to 23 m)

Leaves: Scale-like; bluish green to grayish green; 0.1 to 0.2 inches (0.2 to 0.5 cm) long

Seed Cones: Round; green to gray or grayish brown; 1 inch (2.5 cm) wide

North American Range: Southwestern United States and northern Mexico

Habitat: Dry canyons, stream banks, and rocky slopes

Seed cones

WILDFIRE AND SEED CONES

Some conifers bear thick seed cones that are sealed with resin. The cones may stay closed for years. Heat from a wildfire melts the resin. Then the cones open and release the seeds inside. Trees likely developed this trait so new trees could quickly grow after a wildfire.

BALD CYPRESS

(TAXODIUM DISTICHUM)

The bald cypress is a deciduous conifer that often lives for up to 600 years. Its feathery, needle-like leaves shed each fall. The sage green leaves turn tan, brown, and copper before falling. The bald cypress is known for having knobs around the main trunk that stick out from its roots. These knobs are sometimes called knees. The bald cypress grows well in wet areas. The heavy wood in the tree's core is resistant to rot.

HOW TO SPOT

Height: 80 to 120 feet (24 to 37 m)

Leaves: Needle-like; green to brown; 0.4 to 0.75 inches (1 to 2 cm) long

Seed Cones: Round; green to brown; 0.5 to 1.5 inches (1.3 to 4 cm) wide

North American Range: Southeastern United States

Habitat: Dry areas and riverbanks, swamps, and wetlands

Seed cones

FUN FACT

In the southern United States, the bald cypress grows in swampy water. A plant called Spanish moss often hangs from it.

GOWEN CYPRESS

(HESPEROCYPARIS GOVENIANA)

The Gowen cypress is a rare tree and an endangered species. It grows in only a few coastal areas of central and northwestern California. It can grow tall, but it is more often shrubby. It has a cone or oval shape. Small, scale-like leaves grow on rounded shoots. The leaves have a lemon scent. The seed cones stay closed until their branch dies from wildfire. The seeds inside drop to the ground, which is now clear due to fire.

Seed cones

HOW TO SPOT

Height: 3 to 165 feet (1 to 50 m)

Leaves: Scale-like; bright or dark green; 0.04 to 0.4 inches (0.1 to 1 cm) long

Seed Cones: Round; brown or grayish green; 0.6 to 0.75 inches (1.5 to 2 cm) wide

North American Range: Central California coast

Habitat: Dry and rocky slopes along the coast

LAWSON'S CYPRESS

(CHAMAECYPARIS LAWSONIANA)

The Lawson's cypress grows in a narrow pyramid shape. Its short branches reach upward. Its leaves are flat and scale-like. The leaves have white markings on their undersides that look like small Xs. The leaves smell similar to parsley when crushed. The Lawson's cypress's thick bark helps protect it from wildfires. It is resistant to insect damage too. However, the roots can be damaged by a fungus that causes rot.

HOW TO SPOT

Height: 40 to 180 feet (12 to 55 m) or taller

Leaves: Scale-like; dark green; 0.1 inches (0.2 cm) long

Seed Cones: Round; bluish green to brown; 0.3 inches (0.8 cm) wide

North American Range: Southwestern Oregon and northwestern California

Habitat: Coasts, along streams, and in bogs

FUN FACT

Oil from the Lawson's cypress is used to make natural insect repellents for people.

Seed cones

LEYLAND CYPRESS

(CUPRESSOCYPARIS LEYLANDII)

The Leyland cypress is a hybrid species. It is a mix of Monterey cypress and Nootka cypress. Its seed cones have eight scales each. The seeds inside the cones are sterile. People use cuttings to produce new trees. The tree's branches form a cone or column shape. Small, scale-like leaves grow in thick layers. The bark is scaly and reddish brown. Leyland cypress trees have shallow roots. They do not grow well in hot climates.

HOW TO SPOT

Height: 35 to 50 feet (11 to 15 m)

Leaves: Scale-like; green or bluish green; 0.06 to 2 inches (0.15 to 5 cm) long

Seed Cones: Round; dark brown; 0.4 to 0.75 inches (1 to 2 cm) wide

North American Range: No natural range, but cultivated throughout the United States

Habitat: Grows well in a variety of soil types

Seed cones

MACNAB CYPRESS

(HESPEROCYPARIS MACNABIANA)

The MacNab cypress stands as a small tree or large shrub. It often has multiple trunks. This cypress grows in a spreading shape, often growing wider than it is tall. Small, scale-like leaves grow on the branches. They are dull gray or grayish green in color. Each leaf has a dot filled with resin. Seed cones open from high heat, such as during wildfires. The cones may stay on the trees for years before opening. The tree's reddish-gray to brown bark is fibrous. The MacNab cypress has a spicy scent.

HOW TO SPOT

Height: 10 to 35 feet (3 to 11 m)

Leaves: Scale-like; dull gray or grayish green; 0.1 to 0.4 inches (0.2 to 1 cm) long

Seed Cones: Round; gray to reddish brown; 0.6 to 0.75 inches (1.5 to 2 cm) wide

North American Range: California

Habitat: Dry flats and slopes, chaparral, and woodlands

MONTEREY CYPRESS

(HESPEROCYPARIS MACROCARPA)

The Monterey cypress grows along the coast of central California. It flourishes in climates with a cool coastal breeze. It is one of the largest cypress species, growing up to 90 feet (27 m) tall. A young tree has needle-like leaves and a narrow pyramid shape. A mature tree has thick, scale-like leaves and pale reddish-brown or gray bark with furrows. The leaves have a lemon scent. Many Monterey cypress trees have been cut down to make room for buildings.

HOW TO SPOT

Height: 30 to 90 feet (9 to 27 m)

Leaves: Scale-like; bright to dark green; 0.1 to 0.4 inches (0.2 to 1 cm) long

Seed Cones: Round or oval; green to brown; 1 to 1.5 inches (2.5 to 4 cm) wide

North American Range: Monterey Peninsula, California

Habitat: Cool and dry coastal areas

FUN FACT

A famous Monterey cypress known as the Lone Cypress grows alone out of a rocky cliff in Pebble Beach, California. It is thought to be one of the most photographed trees in the United States.

NOOTKA CYPRESS

(CALLITROPSIS NOOTKATENSIS)

The Nootka cypress grows in the coastal mountains of the Pacific Northwest. Its common name comes from the Nootka Sound in British Columbia, Canada. The Nootka cypress has drooping branches. Its bluish-green leaves are small and scale-like. They grow in flat sprays. The seed cones are berry-like when young. They ripen to be woody and brown with four to six pointy scales. The tree's long-lasting yellow wood is used for timber.

HOW TO SPOT

Height: 30 to 90 feet (9 to 27 m)

Leaves: Scale-like; dark bluish or grayish green; 0.12 to 0.25 inches (0.3 to 0.6 cm) long

Seed Cones: Round; green or bluish green to brown; 0.4 inches (1 cm) wide

North American Range: British Columbia, Canada, and US states of Alaska, Washington, Oregon, and California

Habitat: Coastal mountains and moist soil along streams or ravines

FUN FACT

The study of trees is called dendrology.

Seed cones

NORTHERN WHITECEDAR

(THUJA OCCIDENTALIS)

The northern whitecedar has a large trunk. Its bark is grayish to reddish brown and shreds off in strips. The tree grows in a column or cone shape. Its leaves are fragrant and scale-like. The leaves turn yellowish green in winter. The Ojibwe, the Kitigan Zibi Anishinabeg, and other Indigenous peoples used the tree's lightweight wood to build canoes. The northern whitecedar was one of the first North American trees introduced to Europe. Its scientific name *occidentalis* means "from the Western world."

HOW TO SPOT

Height: 40 to 120 feet (12 to 37 m)

Leaves: Scale-like; yellowish green to grayish green and brown; up to 0.25 inches (0.6 cm) long

Seed Cones: Oval; green to brown; 0.5 inches (1.3 cm) wide

North American Range: Central and eastern Canada and north-central and eastern United States

Habitat: Swamp or lake areas and rocky hillsides

TREE OF LIFE

The northern whitecedar has high amounts of vitamin C. American Indians used parts of the tree to make tea, which helped treat scurvy. This disease is caused by a lack of vitamin C. The Iroquois people passed this information on to Europeans. In the 1530s, French sailors were sick with scurvy. They were cured after drinking tea from the Iroquois people. The story led to the northern whitecedar's other common name of *arborvitae*. This word means "tree of life" in Latin.

SANTA CRUZ CYPRESS

(HESPEROCYPARIS ABRAMSIANA)

The Santa Cruz cypress was first identified as a species in 1948. The rare, pyramid-shaped tree has bright green, scale-like leaves. Its gray bark peels off in strips. Its seed cones have eight to ten scales each. The cones open with heat from wildfires. They may also dry out with age and then release their seeds. The Santa Cruz cypress faces increased threats from habitat loss and wildfires. These threats have led to its status as a threatened species.

Seed cones

HOW TO SPOT

Height: 15 to 33 feet (5 to 10 m)

Leaves: Scale-like; bright green; 0.04 to 0.08 inches (0.1 to 0.2 cm) long

Seed Cones: Round or oval; green to brown; 0.6 to 1.2 inches (1.5 to 3 cm) wide

North American Range: Santa Cruz Mountains in California

Habitat: Sandy and chaparral areas

SARGENT CYPRESS

(HESPEROCYPARIS SARGENTII)

The Sargent cypress grows primarily in California. It is often found growing in serpentine soil on foggy mountain ridges. This type of soil is coarse, rocky, and dry. Fog provides moisture the Sargent cypress needs to survive. The tree is often short and shrub-like. It may be flat and spread wide when growing in windy conditions. But in good soil conditions it can grow up to 90 feet (27 m) tall, forming a round or pyramid shape. The trunk has thick, fibrous, grayish-brown bark. Seed cones open during wildfires.

HOW TO SPOT

Height: 33 to 90 feet (10 to 27 m)

Leaves: Scale-like; gray green to dark green; 0.1 to 0.4 inches (0.2 to 1 cm) long

Seed Cones: Round; brown to gray; 0.6 to 1 inch (1.5 to 2.5 cm) wide

North American Range: Areas of Oregon and California

Habitat: Coastal ranges, foothills and slopes, foggy ridges, and chaparral

SMOOTH ARIZONA CYPRESS

(HESPEROCYPARIS GLABRA)

The Arizona cypress grows in the southwestern United States. It is a hardy tree. It grows in dry and rocky soils and flourishes in hot sun. The tree often has more than one trunk. It has smooth, reddish-brown outer bark that sheds in thin flakes to show bright red inner bark. The scale-like, bluish-green leaves often have small white dots. These are resin glands. After two years, the leaves die. They turn a reddish-brown color. They drop from the tree about four years after they die.

HOW TO SPOT

Height: 20 to 70 feet (6 to 21 m)

Leaves: Scale-like; bright bluish green to reddish brown; 0.1 inches (0.2 cm) long

Seed Cones: Round or oval; gray to brown; 1 inch (2.5 cm) wide

North American Range: Southwestern United States into Mexico

Habitat: Mountains, canyon valleys, and chaparral

Seed cones

BIGCONE DOUGLAS-FIR

(PSEUDOTSUGA MACROCARPA)

The bigcone Douglas-fir grows in the mountains of southern California. The tree begins to bear cones after 50 years. Its large, upright seed cones grow up to seven inches (18 cm) in length and have pointy scales. This fir tree has stiff, needle-like leaves. Its branches grow in the shape of a cone. The bark can be up to eight inches (20 cm) thick. Its thickness helps protect the tree from fire damage. The bark has deep ridges and thin plates.

FUN FACT

Douglas-fir trees are similar to firs, spruces, pines, and hemlocks. In 1867, scientists put the Douglas-fir into its own genus, *Pseudotsuga*. The name means "false hemlock."

Seed cone

HOW TO SPOT

Height: 50 to 100 feet (15 to 30 m)

Leaves: Needle-like; light to dark green; two white bands on undersides; 1.25 to 3 inches (3 to 8 cm) long

Seed Cones: Egg shaped or cylindrical; dark brown; up to 7 inches (18 cm) long

North American Range: Southern California

Habitat: Slopes, cliffs, canyons, and forests

DOUGLAS-FIR *(PSEUDOTSUGA MENZIESII)*

The Douglas-fir grows from British Columbia, Canada, to central California in the United States. In the wild it can grow more than 300 feet (91 m) tall. Its seed cones have rounded scales. Unlike some other conifers, the tree's seed cones have three-pointed bracts. These are inner scales that stick out between the outer scales. The bracts are sometimes known as mousetails because of their shape. The Douglas-fir's needle-like dark green leaves are fragrant. Its lower branches droop as it gets older.

HOW TO SPOT

Height: 40 to 300 feet (12 to 91 m)

Leaves: Needle-like; yellowish green to dark green with two white lines on undersides; 0.75 to 1.25 inches (2 to 3 cm) long

Seed Cones: Oval or cone shaped; light brown; 3 to 4 inches (8 to 10 cm) long

North American Range: Western Canada and United States

Habitat: Coastal areas, foothills, and mountain ranges

Seed cone

WHITE MARKINGS

Many conifers have white lines or bands on their leaves. These are groups of pores, or openings, called stomata. Most plants have thousands of these pores on their surfaces. The pores help the plant take in carbon dioxide and release oxygen during photosynthesis.

FIR FAMILY

BALSAM FIR *(ABIES BALSAMEA)*

The balsam fir's common name refers to resin, also known as balsam. The tree's grayish-brown bark is thin, smooth, and covered with resin-filled blisters. The resin is clear and sticky. The tree's bark becomes scaly with age. The balsam fir grows well in cool climates with lots of moisture. It has flat, shiny, needle-like leaves. Seed cones stand upright on branches. They have short bracts hidden by closed scales, which drop off with age. The fragrant balsam fir is one of the most popular kinds of Christmas trees. It keeps its needles long after the trunk is cut.

HOW TO SPOT

Height: 50 to 90 feet (15 to 27 m)

Leaves: Needle-like; up to 1 inch (2.5 cm) long; deep green with two white lines on undersides

Seed Cones: Cylindrical; purplish; 2.5 to 4 inches (6 to 10 cm) long

North American Range: Southeastern Canada and northeastern United States

Habitat: Cool climates, especially in swamps and forests and on slopes and mountains

Seed cones

BRISTLECONE FIR *(ABIES BRACTEATA)*

The bristlecone fir is a rare conifer. It has a narrow, spiky shape. Its branches often droop slightly. The tree's common name refers to needle-like bracts on its cones. The bracts are about one inch (2.5 cm) long and stick out from between the cone's scales. The tree's needle-like leaves are dark green with pointed tips. Its thin bark has blisters filled with resin. The bark and low branches are highly flammable, so the tree flourishes only in places unlikely to have wildfires.

HOW TO SPOT

Height: 65 to 115 feet (20 to 35 m)

Leaves: Needle-like; dark green; 1.5 to 2.5 inches (4 to 6 cm) long

Seed Cones: Egg shaped; golden to purplish brown; 2.5 to 3.5 inches (6 to 9 cm) long

North American Range: Santa Lucia mountains in California

Habitat: Cool, moist, rocky areas, especially on slopes and in canyons

FRASER FIR *(ABIES FRASERI)*

The Fraser fir grows in the southern Appalachian Mountains above elevations of 4,500 feet (1,370 m). The tree's trunk can be up to two feet (0.6 m) across. Its needle-like leaves are known for their fragrant scent, making the Fraser fir a popular Christmas tree. Its upright cones have long bracts that bend downward. The cones fall apart to release seeds. The bark has blisters filled with resin.

HOW TO SPOT

Height: 30 to 75 feet (9 to 23 m)

Leaves: Needle-like; silvery green to dark green with two white bands on undersides; 0.5 to 1 inch (1.3 to 2.5 cm) long

Seed Cones: Cylindrical; purplish brown; 2.5 inches (6 cm) long

North American Range: Southern Appalachian Mountains in the United States

Habitat: Cold, moist, mountainous areas

GRAND FIR *(ABIES GRANDIS)*

The grand fir is a large tree in its genus. It grows quickly and forms a cone shape with drooping branches. The flat, shiny, needle-like leaves are dark green with silvery-white undersides. The leaves alternate between short and long. They have a citrus scent when crushed. The furrowed bark reveals reddish-brown inner bark. The upright seed cones have short bracts inside.

HOW TO SPOT

Height: 130 to 250 feet (40 to 76 m)

Leaves: Needle-like; glossy dark green with two white bands on undersides; 1 inch (2.5 cm) long

Seed Cones: Cylindrical; brownish green; 1.25 to 4 inches (3 to 10 cm) long

North American Range: British Columbia, Canada, and US states of Washington, Oregon, Idaho, Montana, and California

Habitat: Coastal regions and low elevations

Cones

FIR FAMILY

JALISCO FIR *(ABIES FLINCKII)*

The Jalisco fir is a rare conifer. It grows in Mexico's western state of Jalisco. It has long, needle-like leaves. The tree's bark is a silvery gray. It is smooth when the tree is young and becomes scaly with age. The seed cones are oval or conical. *Abies flinckii* is a similar species to *Abies jaliscana*. Both species are known by the common name of Jalisco fir. Today some Jalisco fir trees grow in protected areas, but illegal logging remains a threat to the species.

HOW TO SPOT

Height: 50 to 115 feet (15 to 35 m)

Leaves: Needle-like; green; 1.5 to 3 inches (4 to 8 cm) long

Seed Cones: Oval or cone shaped; greenish yellow to yellowish brown; 4.5 to 6 inches (11 to 15 cm) long

North American Range: Western and central Mexico

Habitat: Warm forests and mountain ranges

NOBLE FIR *(ABIES PROCERA)*

The noble fir grows along the northwestern Pacific Coast of the United States. Its scientific name means "tall tree" in Latin. It is the tallest true fir and can grow to more than 270 feet (82 m) tall. Its trunk may reach up to 28 feet (8.5 m) around. The tree's short branches may not start until 100 feet (30 m) up the trunk. A young tree's bark is smooth and gray with resin-filled blisters. The bark turns rough and dark red with age. The needle-like leaves have a slight curve at their base. The noble fir is a common Christmas tree.

Seed cones

HOW TO SPOT

Height: 50 to 270 feet (15 to 82 m) or taller

Leaves: Needle-like; bluish green with white markings; 1 to 1.5 inches (2.5 to 4 cm) long

Seed Cones: Cylindrical; purplish brown; 5.5 to 10 inches (14 to 25 cm) long

North American Range: Washington, Oregon, and California

Habitat: Mountain forests

PACIFIC SILVER FIR *(ABIES AMABILIS)*

The Pacific silver fir is common throughout the Pacific Northwest. It flourishes in the cool temperatures of high elevations, although it can also grow in warmer temperatures at lower elevations along coastlines. The Pacific fir lives for approximately 400 years. Its seed cones grow upright. They fall apart with age to release winged seeds. The tree's flat, needle-like leaves are dark green with silver or white lines on their undersides. The silvery color of these markings gives the tree its common name.

HOW TO SPOT

Height: 150 to 260 feet (46 to 79 m)

Leaves: Needle-like; dark green with two white or silver lines on undersides; 1 to 3 inches (2.5 to 8 cm) long

Seed Cones: Oval; purplish gray to brown; 3.5 to 6.5 inches (9 to 17 cm) long

North American Range: Pacific Northwest of Canada and the United States

Habitat: Coastal regions, mountain ranges, and valleys

FUN FACT

Some American Indian peoples, such as the Ditidaht, chewed the resin of the Pacific silver fir tree as gum. They used the branches for bedding or floor coverings.

RED FIR *(ABIES MAGNIFICA)*

The red fir grows in forests along the western Sierra Nevada range. It has short, horizontal branches that form a narrow pyramid shape. The tree has smooth, gray bark with resin blisters. It develops rare orangish-red or reddish-brown bark as it ages. The bark also develops furrows with wide ridges. The red fir has needle-like, bluish-green leaves. The leaves curve to make a slight S shape. The tree's scientific name, *magnifica*, means "magnificent."

HOW TO SPOT

Height: 60 to 200 feet (18 to 61 m)

Leaves: Needle-like; bluish green with white lines on both sides; 0.75 to 1.25 inches (2 to 3 cm) long

Seed Cones: Cylindrical; purplish brown to brown; 6 to 9 inches (15 to 23 cm) long

North American Range: Oregon and California

Habitat: Dry mountain slopes and ridges

Seed cones

FIR FAMILY

SUBALPINE FIR *(ABIES LASIOCARPA)*

The subalpine fir has a narrow column or pyramid shape with short, dense branches that droop slightly. Its bark splits as it ages. Purplish-brown seed cones grow upright in groups along the branches. In fall the cones break apart and release winged seeds. When subalpine firs grow on mountain slopes, their roots protect the soil from wearing away.

HOW TO SPOT

Height: 20 to 90 feet (6 to 27 m)

Leaves: Needle-like; bluish green to grayish green with white bands; 1 to 1.5 inches (2.5 to 4 cm) long

Seed Cones: Cylindrical; purple to brown or black; 1.5 to 4 inches (4 to 10 cm) long

North American Range: Alaska, western Canada, and western United States

Habitat: Cool, wet forests

FUN FACT

Corkbark fir is a variety of subalpine fir found in the Rocky Mountains. Its whitish bark has the texture of cork.

WHITE FIR *(ABIES CONCOLOR)*

The white fir grows in mountain ranges in the western United States. It has short, flat, needle-like leaves that are some of the longest leaves among fir trees. The underside of each leaf is white. The leaves have a citrus scent when crushed. When young, the white fir grows in a pyramid shape. The tree grows into a dome shape as it ages. An adult white fir has scaly, gray bark with deep furrows. The white fir is commonly used as a Christmas tree.

HOW TO SPOT

Height: 40 to 180 feet (12 to 55 m)

Leaves: Needle-like; silvery to bluish green; 1.5 to 2.5 inches (4 to 6 cm) long

Seed Cones: Oval and upright; green to brown; 3 to 5 inches (8 to 13 cm) long

North American Range: Western United States

Habitat: Mountain slopes and rocky areas

Seed cones

CAROLINA HEMLOCK

(TSUGA CAROLINIANA)

The slow-growing Carolina hemlock grows in the Appalachian Mountains. It has a pyramid shape with short branches that may droop downward. Its needle-like leaves are dark green with two white lines on the underside of each. The leaves stick out evenly around the stem. They smell similar to a tangerine when crushed. The tree's reddish-brown bark has scaly ridges. The Cherokee people used the Carolina hemlock for medicine, making baskets, and building. This species is threatened by pests.

Leaves with pest infection

HOW TO SPOT

Height: 40 to 95 feet (12 to 29 m)

Leaves: Needle-like; green with white lines on undersides; 0.25 to 0.75 inches (0.6 to 2 cm) long

Seed Cones: Egg shaped or oval; green to light brown; 1 to 1.5 inches (2.5 to 4 cm) long with narrow scales

North American Range: Southeastern United States

Habitat: Dry slopes, cliffs, and rocky areas

PEST THREATS

Conifers face threats from pests such as bagworms, beetles, aphids, mites, and moths. The hemlock woolly adelgid is a deadly pest for hemlock trees. This invasive insect from Asia feeds on sap. This damages the tree and keeps it from getting the nutrients it needs. Sick trees have white egg sacs on their branches. The sacs resemble tufts of cotton.

EASTERN HEMLOCK

(TSUGA CANADENSIS)

The eastern hemlock is also known as the Canada hemlock or hemlock spruce. The pyramid-shaped tree grows slowly, but it can live for 800 years or more. The needle-like leaves grow on drooping, feathery branches. Two pale bands on the underside of each leaf give the trees a silvery look. The eastern hemlock is sometimes mistaken for the Carolina hemlock. However, the eastern hemlock's leaves are lighter in color and longer than those of the Carolina hemlock.

FUN FACT

The hemlock's genus name, *Tsuga*, comes from the Japanese words for "tree" and "mother."

HOW TO SPOT

Height: 40 to 100 feet (12 to 30 m)

Leaves: Needle-like; glossy green with white undersides; 0.5 inches (1.3 cm) long

Seed Cones: Egg shaped; green to brown; up to 1 inch (2.5 cm) long

North American Range: Eastern Canada and north-central and eastern United States

Habitat: Cool, humid places, including rocky ridges and hills, mountain slopes, and near streams

MOUNTAIN HEMLOCK

(TSUGA MERTENSIANA)

The mountain hemlock grows as a low shrub at high altitudes. In low altitudes it grows as a tall tree with a narrow cone or pyramid shape. Its branches may grow twisted in windy areas. The tree's needle-like leaves may be bluish green, gray, or silver. They form star-like groups on each branch. The mountain hemlock has a flexible trunk that can bend under the weight of snow. Once the snow melts, the tree stands upright again.

HOW TO SPOT

Height: 15 to 100 feet (5 to 30 m)

Leaves: Needle-like; grayish green to silvery white with white lines on both sides; 0.5 to 0.75 inches (1.3 to 2 cm) long

Seed Cones: Cylindrical; purple to brown; 2 to 3 inches (5 to 8 cm) long

North American Range: Western Canada and United States, from Alaska to California

Habitat: Mountain slopes and moist areas

WESTERN HEMLOCK

(TSUGA HETEROPHYLLA)

The western hemlock grows throughout the Pacific Northwest from Alaska to California. It is the largest hemlock tree. Its leaves are arranged in a spiral around each stem. Its trunk can reach up to nine feet (2.7 m) across. Its bark is reddish brown and scaly. The western hemlock begins producing cones when it is 25 to 30 years old. Each cone has 30 to 40 seeds.

Seed cones

HOW TO SPOT

Height: 100 to 200 feet (30 to 61 m) or taller

Leaves: Needle-like; dark green; 0.25 to 0.75 inches (0.6 to 2 cm) long

Seed Cones: Oval; purple to light brown; 0.6 to 1 inch (1.5 to 2.5 cm) long

North American Range: Pacific Coast and Rocky Mountains of Canada and the United States

Habitat: Coasts, humid and foggy areas, and moist stream bottoms

ANCIENT PLANTS

Conifers have grown on Earth for more than 300 million years. They grew before flowering plants existed. Many plant-eating dinosaurs ate conifers. Scientists study fossils of conifers to learn more about prehistoric times.

ALLIGATOR JUNIPER

(JUNIPERUS DEPPEANA)

The alligator juniper is one of the largest junipers in the southwestern United States. The scale-like leaves are dark bluish green. The tree has a fragrant scent. Male and female cones usually grow on separate trees. The alligator juniper is known for its bark, which resembles alligator skin. It sheds in thick, checkered plates. Dead branches remain on the tree rather than falling off as the tree ages. This tree provides an important habitat for wildlife.

HOW TO SPOT

Height: 20 to 65 feet (6 to 20 m)

Leaves: Scale-like; bluish green; about 0.06 inches (0.15 cm) long

Seed Cones: Round and berry-like; reddish brown with waxy coating; 0.25 to 0.5 inches (0.6 to 1.3 cm) wide

North American Range: Southwestern United States and northern and central Mexico

Habitat: Mountains, rocky hills, and slopes

ASHE JUNIPER *(JUNIPERUS ASHEI)*

The Ashe juniper grows as a small tree or large shrub. It has an uneven shape and twisted trunk. Its scale-like leaves have a fragrant cedar scent, which comes from resin glands on the leaves. The glands also make the tree resistant to decay and bugs. This species has separate male and female trees. Blue, berry-like cones grow on female trees. Male trees turn golden brown in winter from their cones' pollen.

HOW TO SPOT

Height: 15 to 30 feet (5 to 9 m)

Leaves: Scale-like; bluish green; 0.12 inches (0.3 cm) long

Seed Cones: Round and berry-like; dark blue; 0.2 to 0.4 inches (0.5 to 1 cm) wide

North American Range: US states of Texas, Oklahoma, Missouri, and Arkansas and northern Mexico

Habitat: Canyons and open areas of limestone

Seed cones

FUN FACT

The rare golden-cheeked warbler builds its nest in Ashe juniper trees.

BERMUDA JUNIPER

(JUNIPERUS BERMUDIANA)

The Bermuda juniper grows on the island territory of Bermuda. It is also known as the Bermuda red cedar. A young Bermuda juniper tree has thin, flaky, dark red bark. The bark turns grayish brown with age and peels off in long strips. Each cone contains one or two (rarely three) seeds. The Bermuda juniper is critically endangered, but people have led large conservation efforts in recent years. The tree's population is starting to recover.

HOW TO SPOT

Height: Up to 50 feet (15 m)

Leaves: Scale-like; grayish green to bluish green; 0.04 to 0.1 inches (0.1 to 0.2 cm) wide

Seed Cones: Round and berry-like; dark blue with waxy coating; about 0.2 inches (0.5 cm) wide

North American Range: Bermuda

Habitat: Hillsides, marshes, and coastlines

CALIFORNIA JUNIPER

(JUNIPERUS CALIFORNICA)

The California juniper grows as a small tree or shrub. It grows in California and other places with mild winters and hot, dry summers. A young tree's leaves are needle-like, but the tree develops scale-like leaves as it matures. The tree grows crooked and uneven. It usually has multiple trunks with thin, peeling, gray bark. Male and female cones usually grow on separate trees.

HOW TO SPOT

Height: 3 to 25 feet (1 to 8 m)

Leaves: Scale-like; light green to bluish gray; 0.04 to 0.1 inches (0.1 to 0.2 cm) long

Seed Cones: Round and berry-like; blue to reddish brown with waxy coating; 0.3 to 0.5 inches (0.8 to 1.3 cm) wide

North American Range: US states of California, Nevada, and Arizona and Baja California, Mexico

Habitat: Dry slopes, desert scrublands and chaparral, and open woodlands

FUN FACT

The California juniper provides food and shelter for wildlife, including deer, elk, and wild horses.

CHINESE JUNIPER

(JUNIPERUS CHINENSIS)

The Chinese juniper is native to China, Japan, Mongolia, and the Himalayas in Asia. In North America people cultivate many varieties of this species. That means people plant the tree for landscaping. The Chinese juniper may grow as a tree, shrub, or ground cover. Its flat, scale-like leaves have a fragrant scent. The brown bark peels away in narrow strips. Seed cones are fleshy and berry-like. They are whitish blue at first. They become purplish brown with age. The Chinese juniper is commonly used for bonsai, an Asian art. In bonsai a person grows and shapes a tiny tree so that it resembles a full-sized tree.

HOW TO SPOT

Height: 40 to 70 feet (12 to 21 m)

Leaves: Scale-like; dark green; 1 to 3 inches (2.5 to 8 cm) long

Seed Cones: Round and berry-like; whitish blue to purplish brown; 0.5 inches (1.3 cm) wide

North American Range: Cultivated throughout North America

Habitat: Sunny places with dry soil; cultivated varieties grow in several soil types

COMITÁN JUNIPER

(JUNIPERUS COMITANA)

The Comitán juniper grows from Comitán in southern Mexico to northern Guatemala. It generally grows at elevations of 4,270 to 5,910 feet (1,300 to 1,800 m). It has a single trunk that may branch off. Its bark can be gray, red, or brown and peels away in long strips. Male and female cones grow on separate trees. The Comitán juniper is endangered because of habitat loss and deforestation. The tree is used for agriculture and timber.

HOW TO SPOT

Height: Up to 33 feet (10 m)

Leaves: Scale-like; bright green; about 0.1 inches (0.2 cm) long

Seed Cones: Round and berry-like; dark blue; 0.2 to 0.4 inches (0.5 to 1 cm) wide

North American Range: Southern Mexico and northern Guatemala

Habitat: Dry, rocky slopes; canyons; and woodlands

JUNIPER FAMILY

COMMON JUNIPER

(JUNIPERUS COMMUNIS)

The common juniper may grow as ground cover, a shrub, or a tree. Its size and shape depend on location and temperature. In the United States the common juniper most often grows as a low shrub with multiple trunks. It has the widest range of any conifer. Unlike most other junipers, its leaves are needle-like. They grow in groups of three. Male and female cones grow on separate trees. The seed cones are known as juniper berries. The tree's bark is reddish brown and sheds in strips.

HOW TO SPOT

Height: 9 inches to 50 feet (0.2 to 15 m)

Leaves: Needle-like; dark green to brownish with a white band on the upper side; 0.25 to 0.5 inches (0.6 to 1.3 cm) long

Seed Cones: Round and berry-like; green to dark blue or black with waxy coating; 0.5 inches (1.3 cm) wide

North American Range: Canada and northern United States, including Alaska

Habitat: Forests, open alpine areas, plains, and sandy or rocky areas

Seed cones

JUNIPER BERRIES

The common juniper is well known for its seed cones, also called juniper berries. People rarely eat these berries raw because they have a strong, bitter taste similar to pine. Instead, people mix the berries into foods and drinks. They also dry and crush them for soups and marinades.

CREEPING JUNIPER

(JUNIPERUS HORIZONTALIS)

The creeping juniper gets its name from its wide-spreading, low growth. It often grows less than one foot (0.3 m) tall. It spreads up to ten feet (3 m) wide. The branches form a mat over dry or sandy soil. Adult creeping juniper trees have soft, scale-like leaves that are bluish green to green. They may turn purple in winter. The tree's bark is dark to reddish brown and peeling. Male and female cones grow on separate trees. People often plant creeping juniper in rock gardens or as ground cover.

HOW TO SPOT

Height: 0.5 to 1.5 feet (0.2 to 0.5 m)

Leaves: Scale-like; purplish to bluish green or green; 0.04 to 0.12 inches (0.1 to 0.3 cm) long

Seed Cones: Round and berry-like; green to blue; 0.2 to 0.4 inches (0.5 to 1 cm) wide

North American Range: Canada and northern United States, including Alaska

Habitat: Prairies; rocky, sandy soil; and rocky slopes or cliffs

JUNIPER FAMILY

DURANGO JUNIPER

(JUNIPERUS DURANGENSIS)

The Durango juniper is a shrub or small tree. Its range includes the Mexican states of Aguascalientes, Chihuahua, Durango, Jalisco, Sonora, and Zacatecas. The Durango juniper has dark red bark. The bark may be smooth or peel in long strips. Durango juniper branches reach upward to form an uneven canopy.

HOW TO SPOT

Height: Up to 15 feet (5 m)

Leaves: Scale-like; dark grayish green; 0.04 to 0.1 inches (0.1 to 0.2 cm) long

Seed Cones: Round and berry-like; 0.2 to 0.25 inches (0.5 to 0.6 cm) wide

North American Range: Northern to central Mexico

Habitat: Pine forests

EASTERN RED JUNIPER

(JUNIPERUS VIRGINIANA)

The eastern red juniper is native to 37 US states. It can grow in many places, from swamps to dry, rocky areas. Its scale-like leaves can be various shades of green. The tree's fragrant, soft bark is reddish brown to gray. It is resistant to rot and insects. The bark sheds in long, thin strips to show gray inner bark. The seed cones turn from green to blue as they age. Several animals eat these cones. The male cones are smaller and yellow.

HOW TO SPOT

Height: 10 to 90 feet (3 to 27 m)

Leaves: Scale-like; bluish green; up to 1.5 inches (4 cm) long

Seed Cones: Round and berry-like; blue with waxy coating; 0.25 inches (0.6 cm) wide

North American Range: Southeastern Canada and eastern United States

Habitat: Prairies, plains, meadows, and swamps

GAMBOA JUNIPER

(JUNIPERUS GAMBOANA)

The Gamboa juniper grows in Mexico. Its branches reach upward to form a round canopy. The bark is grayish brown. The Gamboa juniper has some similar traits to the alligator juniper, such as scaly bark that sheds in thick plates. Habitat loss has been a main threat to the Gamboa juniper, leading to its status as an endangered species.

HOW TO SPOT

Height: Up to 40 feet (12 m)

Leaves: Scale-like; yellowish green to green; 0.06 to 0.1 inches (0.15 to 0.2 cm) long

Seed Cones: Round and berry-like; reddish brown with waxy coating; 0.2 to 0.3 inches (0.5 to 0.8 cm) wide

North American Range: Southern Mexico

Habitat: Limestone soils and open pine forests

JALISCO JUNIPER

(JUNIPERUS JALISCANA)

The Jalisco juniper grows in Mexico's states of Durango and Jalisco. This rare tree has a round or cone shape. Its bark is grayish brown and shreds in strips to reveal reddish-brown inner bark. The leaves are scale-like with very fine teeth. The Jalisco juniper is endangered. It experiences habitat loss when humans clear land for farming, ranching, or other uses.

HOW TO SPOT

Height: Up to 33 feet (10 m)

Leaves: Scale-like; green; 0.04 inches (0.1 cm) long

Seed Cones: Round and berry-like; reddish brown with waxy coating; about 0.3 inches (0.8 cm) wide

North American Range: Northwestern and southern Mexico

Habitat: Hillsides, slopes, and grassy areas

MEXICAN WEEPING JUNIPER

(JUNIPERUS FLACCIDA)

The slow-growing Mexican weeping juniper is a large shrub or small tree. It is known for its drooping or weeping branches. This juniper grows from western Texas to southern Mexico in the woodlands and scrub areas of the Chisos Mountains. Its furrowed bark peels away in long, shredded strips. Male and female cones grow on separate trees. Wind blows pollen from male cones to female trees, where the seed cones are pollinated. Each seed cone has between 4 and 12 seeds.

HOW TO SPOT

Height: 25 to 55 feet (8 to 17 m)

Leaves: Scale-like; green to yellowish or brown; 0.06 to 0.1 inches (0.15 to 0.2 cm) long

Seed Cones: Round and berry-like; tan to brownish purple with waxy covering; 0.25 to 0.5 inches (0.6 to 1.3 cm) wide

North American Range: Western Texas in the United States to southern Mexico

Habitat: Rocky or sandy soils and slopes

MOUNTAIN JUNIPER

(JUNIPERUS MONTICOLA)

The mountain juniper is a shrub or small tree. It grows at elevations of 6,560 to 15,420 feet (2,000 to 4,700 m). As a shrub the mountain juniper may sprawl across the ground and form a mat. Its branches are often crooked. The female cones resemble fleshy blue berries. The gray or grayish-brown bark peels off in long, shredded strips.

HOW TO SPOT

Height: Up to 33 feet (10 m)

Leaves: Scale-like; grayish green to green; 0.04 to 0.1 inches (0.1 to 0.2 cm) long

Seed Cones: Round and berry-like; bluish black with waxy coating; 0.2 to 0.6 inches (0.5 to 1.5 cm) wide

North American Range: Mexico

Habitat: Rocky areas, mountain shrubland, and grasslands

JUNIPER FAMILY

ONE-SEED JUNIPER

(JUNIPERUS MONOSPERMA)

The one-seed juniper is a small tree or shrub found in western North America. It often has multiple twisted trunks. Young trees have needle-like leaves that become scaly with age. The tree's bark is thin and scaly. The seed cones look like dark blue berries. Each cone usually has one seed. The one-seed juniper's roots can stretch up to 200 feet (61 m) deep. They help the tree survive in dry climates. The Navajo people made mats and cloth from the tree's wood.

Seed cones

HOW TO SPOT

Height: 6 to 40 feet (1.8 to 12 m)

Leaves: Scale-like; yellowish green to grayish green; 0.6 inches (1.5 cm) long

Seed Cones: Round and berry-like; dark blue to purplish brown with waxy coating; 0.25 inches (0.6 cm) wide

North American Range: Western United States and northern Mexico

Habitat: Slopes or rocky ridges and dry or sandy areas

FUN FACT

The one-seed juniper grows orange flowers that turn into seed cones.

PINCHOT'S JUNIPER

(JUNIPERUS PINCHOTII)

Pinchot's juniper is a shrub or small tree. It often has multiple trunks with thin, scaly, gray bark that sheds in narrow strips. The female cones resemble fleshy berries. Each cone usually has only a single seed. After the tree is cut or burned down, Pinchot's juniper can regrow by sprouting from its stump. Sometimes Pinchot's juniper is called the redberry juniper. However, it is different than *Juniperus coahuilensis*, which has the common name of redberry juniper. The two species look similar. But Pinchot's juniper has seed cones with a deeper reddish-brown color.

HOW TO SPOT

Height: 3 to 25 feet (1 to 8 m)

Leaves: Scale-like; yellowish green; 0.06 to 0.1 inches (0.15 to 0.2 cm) long

Seed Cones: Round and berry-like; reddish brown to deep red; 0.2 to 0.3 inches (0.5 to 0.8 cm) wide

North American Range: Southwestern United States and northeastern Mexico

Habitat: Rocky and dry areas, canyons, slopes, and flats

AN IMPORTANT TREE

Pinchot's juniper is an important source of food and shelter for many kinds of wildlife. The gray vireo is a small desert bird that uses Pinchot's juniper for nesting and roosting. The US state of New Mexico lists the gray vireo as threatened, making Pinchot's juniper an important habitat for the bird.

REDBERRY JUNIPER

(JUNIPERUS COAHUILENSIS)

The redberry juniper grows as a small tree or shrub. It often has multiple trunks with thin, scaly, gray bark that peels off in long, shaggy strips. The inner wood is brown or reddish brown. The spreading branches have scale-like leaves and are often covered in resin. Male and female cones grow on separate trees. The tree's common name comes from its pinkish-red seed cones, which look similar to berries. Deer, birds, livestock, and other animals eat and scatter the seeds during fall.

HOW TO SPOT

Height: 15 to 25 feet (5 to 8 m)

Leaves: Scale-like; grayish green; 0.06 inches (0.15 cm) long

Seed Cones: Round and berry-like; light green to pinkish red; 0.3 inches (0.8 cm) wide

North American Range: Southwestern United States and northern Mexico

Habitat: Desert hills, canyons, grasslands, chaparral, and lowlands

ROCKY MOUNTAIN JUNIPER

(JUNIPERUS SCOPULORUM)

The Rocky Mountain juniper has slightly drooping leaves. A young tree has needle-like leaves, but an adult has scale-like leaves. The tree's green color may have silver or blue tones. Its reddish-brown or gray bark sheds in strips. Male and female cones often grow on separate trees. The berry-like seed cones are dark blue, but they may appear whitish blue when covered in natural wax. The wood has a musty scent. The tree's scientific name means "of the cliffs or rock," which refers to the tree's usual habitat.

HOW TO SPOT

Height: 30 to 65 feet (9 to 20 m)

Leaves: Scale-like; bluish or silvery green; 0.04 to 0.1 inches (0.1 to 0.2 cm) long

Seed Cones: Round and berry-like; green to dark blue with waxy covering; 0.2 to 0.3 inches (0.5 to 0.8 cm) wide

North American Range: Southwestern Canada through the western US Great Plains region

Habitat: Mountains, foothills, slopes, sandy hillsides, and dry, rocky ridges

Seed cones

SALTILLO JUNIPER

(JUNIPERUS SALTILLENSIS)

The Saltillo juniper is a rare shrub or short tree. It is found in the northern Mexican states of Chihuahua, Coahuila, Nuevo León, and Zacatecas. Its name refers to Saltillo, the capital city of Coahuila. It grows at elevations between 5,900 and 9,500 feet (1,800 and 2,900 m). Its thick, gray bark is smooth. The seed cones are dark blue and berry-like. The Saltillo juniper is an endangered species. Threats come from habitat loss, farming, ranching, and the use of its wood.

HOW TO SPOT

Height: Up to 23 feet (7 m)

Leaves: Scale-like; grayish green; 0.02 to 0.06 inches (0.05 to 0.15 cm) long

Seed Cones: Oval or round; berry-like; bluish black with waxy coating; 0.2 to 0.3 inches (0.5 to 0.8 cm) wide

North American Range: Northern Mexico

Habitat: Mountain regions and dry grasslands

SEASIDE JUNIPER

(JUNIPERUS MARITIMA)

The seaside juniper often grows near a sea or lake, but it can also grow on mountain ridges. It has even been found on sand dunes near Washington's Puget Sound. The tree is dark green. Branches grow in an upswept direction. The seaside juniper was once thought to be the same species as the Rocky Mountain juniper. But in 2007 scientists classified the seaside juniper as a separate species due to differences in its seed cones. Seaside juniper seeds often stick out from their cones.

HOW TO SPOT

Height: Up to 65 feet (20 m)

Leaves: Scale-like; green; about 0.1 inches (0.2 cm) long

Seed Cones: Round and berry-like; blue; 0.2 to 0.3 inches (0.5 to 0.8 cm) wide

North American Range: British Columbia, Canada, and Washington, United States

Habitat: Coastal bluffs, rocky areas, shorelines, and mountain ridges

SIERRA JUNIPER *(JUNIPERUS GRANDIS)*

The Sierra juniper grows as a shrub or medium-sized tree. It often grows at elevations of 3,280 to 10,170 feet (1,000 to 3,100 m). The long-living tree is estimated to reach more than 2,500 years in age. The bark of a young Sierra juniper is smooth and pinkish brown. An adult tree's bark is gray to brown. It sheds in thin strips. The tree's scale-like leaves grow in groups of three or four. Usually male and female cones grow on separate trees. The fleshy, berry-like seed cones take two years to mature. Then they dry out and fall off. Animals help scatter the seeds.

HOW TO SPOT

Height: 33 to 85 feet (10 to 26 m)

Leaves: Scale-like; dark green; 0.1 to 0.2 inches (0.2 to 0.5 cm) long

Seed Cones: Round and berry-like; purplish red to blue with waxy coating; 0.2 to 0.4 inches (0.5 to 1 cm) wide

North American Range: Western United States

Habitat: Flats, forests, mountain ranges, and rocky slopes

STANDLEY'S JUNIPER

(JUNIPERUS STANDLEYI)

Standley's juniper is also called *huitó*, *cipres*, and *huitum* in Spanish. The tree is found at elevations of 9,840 to 13,940 feet (3,000 to 4,250 m). It has small, scale-like leaves. Its seed cones are fleshy and berry-like. Each seed cone contains three to six seeds. Its bark peels in long strips. Standley's juniper is an endangered species. Laws protect the species, but many people still cut these trees down. Sheep also eat Standley's juniper, harming its population.

HOW TO SPOT

Height: Up to 50 feet (15 m)

Leaves: Scale-like; yellowish to dark green; 0.06 to 0.1 inches (0.15 to 0.2 cm) long

Seed Cones: Round and berry-like; bluish black with waxy coating; 0.3 to 0.4 inches (0.8 to 1 cm) wide

North American Range: Southeastern Mexico

Habitat: Rocky ridges, mesas, and open woodlands

UTAH JUNIPER

(JUNIPERUS OSTEOSPERMA)

The Utah juniper is a small tree or shrub. It grows throughout the southwestern United States. The tree grows slowly and becomes twisted and ragged with age. It may have several trunks. The top of the plant forms round clumps. Male and female cones grow on each tree. The male cones resemble tiny brown scales at the end of the leaves. The gray to reddish-brown bark is thin and scaly. American Indians, including the Havasupai people, have long used the bark for making mats, bags, sandals, and other items.

Cones

HOW TO SPOT

Height: 10 to 30 feet (3 to 9 m)

Leaves: Scale-like; light green or yellowish green; 0.04 to 0.1 inches (0.1 to 0.2 cm) long

Cones: Berry-like; bluish or reddish brown with waxy coating; 0.2 to 0.3 inches (0.5 to 0.8 cm) wide

North American Range: Western and southwestern United States

Habitat: Canyons, rocky areas, dry plains, and hillsides

WESTERN JUNIPER

(JUNIPERUS OCCIDENTALIS)

The western juniper grows as a tree or shrub. It is found in mountainous regions of the western United States. The slow-growing tree reaches its full height at about 100 years old. It may become twisted with age. The reddish-brown bark is furrowed and shreds. The scale-like leaves are grayish green with white dots of resin. The tree's roots spread out to the sides. Some roots may reach three times the height of the tree underground.

FUN FACT

The oldest known living western juniper grows in Oregon. It is thought to be at least 2,000 years old, but it could be more than 6,000 years old.

Seed cones

HOW TO SPOT

Height: 15 to 100 feet (5 to 30 m)

Leaves: Scale-like; grayish green; 0.04 to 0.1 inches (0.1 to 0.2 cm) long

Seed Cones: Berry-like; blue with waxy coating; 0.2 to 0.4 inches (0.5 to 1 cm) wide

North American Range: Washington, Oregon, Idaho, California, and Nevada

Habitat: Rocky areas, canyons, and valleys

TAMARACK *(LARIX LARICINA)*

The tamarack is a deciduous conifer. Deciduous conifer trees have traits of both deciduous trees, with leaves dropping in fall, and conifers. The tamarack's soft, needle-like leaves change from green to golden yellow in the fall and then drop off the tree. In spring the tree grows new leaves. Small pink cones show through as the leaves grow. This tree grows well in cold climates. Its rough bark has thin, reddish-brown scales. The Algonquin people used tamarack wood to make snowshoes. The Ojibwe used the roots to make canoes. Today the tree's lumber has many uses in construction.

HOW TO SPOT

Height: 40 to 80 feet (12 to 24 m)

Leaves: Needle-like; green or bluish green to yellow; 0.5 to 1 inch (1.3 to 2.5 cm) long

Seed Cones: Oval; brown or maroon; 0.75 inches (2 cm) long

North American Range: Canada and the northern United States, including Alaska

Habitat: Mountain slopes and along streams, lakes, bogs, and swamps

Young seed cones

WESTERN LARCH

(LARIX OCCIDENTALIS)

The western larch is one of the world's tallest larches. It grows up to 270 feet (82 m) tall. The tree grows in a pyramid shape, although most of its trunk may lack branches. The reddish-brown bark of a young tree is scaly. The bark becomes thick and furrowed with age. The western larch is a deciduous conifer. Its soft, needle-like leaves grow in groups of 15 to 30. They are light green and turn golden in fall before they drop. The seed cones of western larch trees have about 30 scales with pointy bract tips.

HOW TO SPOT

Height: 100 to 270 feet (30 to 82 m)

Leaves: Needle-like; pale green to yellow; 1.25 to 2 inches (3 to 5 cm) long

Seed Cones: Oval; reddish brown; 1.25 to 2 inches (3 to 5 cm) long

North American Range: Western Canada and northwestern United States

Habitat: Swamps, mountain slopes, and valleys

FUN FACT

The western larch's natural sugar can be used to make baking powder.

BIG-CONE PINYON

(PINUS MAXIMARTINEZII)

The big-cone pinyon is a small, rare tree. It grows in only two remote locations in northern Mexico. People discovered the first location in Zacatecas in 1964. For decades this was the only known place where the tree grew. In 2010 a Mexican scientist found a second population growing in Durango. The big-cone pinyon is endangered. The tree faces threats from cattle, fire, and humans collecting its seeds, which are eaten as pine nuts. The tree has needle-like leaves that grow in groups of five.

Seed cone

HOW TO SPOT

Height: 20 to 70 feet (6 to 21 m)

Leaves: Needle-like; bluish green; 2.5 to 5 inches (6 to 13 cm) long

Seed Cones: Oval or cylindrical; pale brown; 5.5 to 10 inches (14 to 25 cm) long

North American Range: Durango and Zacatecas, Mexico

Habitat: Rocky mountain slopes

COLORADO PINYON *(PINUS EDULIS)*

The Colorado pinyon commonly grows at elevations of between 5,000 and 8,000 feet (1,520 to 2,440 m). It is also known as the two-leaf pinyon because its needle-like leaves grow in pairs. The slow-growing tree is one of the most drought-resistant pine trees. Its very long roots help it flourish in high, dry places. Its tap root can reach 40 feet (12 m) or more into the soil. This tree produces pine nuts, also called pinyon nuts. These are edible. *Edulis*, part of the tree's scientific name, means "edible" in Latin.

Seed cone

HOW TO SPOT

Height: 10 to 45 feet (3 to 14 m)

Leaves: Needle-like; yellowish green to bluish green with white markings; 2.5 to 4.5 inches (6 to 11 cm) long

Seed Cones: Egg shaped; yellowish brown; 1.5 to 2 inches (4 to 5 cm) long

North American Range: Western and southwestern United States and northern Mexico

Habitat: Mesas, plateaus, rocky areas, and dry mountain slopes

COULTER PINE *(PINUS COULTERI)*

The Coulter pine is also known as a big-cone pine. The tree begins bearing cones at 10 to 15 years old. Its spiny, yellowish-brown seed cones are large and heavy. They weigh four to five pounds (1.8 to 2.3 kg). These are some of the largest cones of any pine tree. Falling cones can be dangerous to people walking underneath the trees. A young Coulter pine bears cones on its trunk before it grows branches. The tree's stiff, needle-like leaves grow in groups of three. The tree's branches reach upward or straight out.

HOW TO SPOT

Height: 30 to 80 feet (9 to 24 m)

Leaves: Needle-like; grayish green with light lines; 6 to 12 inches (15 to 30 cm) long

Seed Cones: Egg shaped; yellowish brown; 8 to 14 inches (20 to 36 cm) long

North American Range: Southern California in the United States and Baja California, Mexico

Habitat: Coastal mountains and warm, dry, rocky slopes and ridges

Seed cone

EASTERN WHITE PINE

(PINUS STROBUS)

The eastern white pine is the largest conifer in the northeastern United States. It is known for its branches that grow in tiers. Its bluish-green, needle-like leaves are soft and flexible. They grow in groups of five. The tree starts producing cones after five to ten years. The eastern white pine was an important tree throughout history for its use as shipbuilding material and for other construction. Today it is used in construction, furniture manufacturing, and millwork.

HOW TO SPOT

Height: 50 to 80 feet (15 to 24 m)

Leaves: Needle-like; bluish green; 2 to 4 inches (5 to 10 cm) long

Seed Cones: Cylindrical; light to dark brown; 3 to 8 inches (8 to 20 cm) long

North American Range: Northeastern Canada and United States

Habitat: Stream banks and high, dry, or rocky ridges

PINE FAMILY

EGG-CONE PINE *(PINUS OOCARPA)*

The egg-cone pine has several common names, including *ocote*, Mexican yellow pine, and hazelnut pine. It has a single trunk. Its needle-like leaves grow in groups of four or five. The thick bark is dark grayish brown. It is rough and scaly with plates of various sizes. The wood of egg-cone pines is often used in construction.

HOW TO SPOT

Height: 50 to 120 feet (15 to 37 m)

Leaves: Needle-like; yellowish green; 8 to 10 inches (20 to 25 cm) long

Seed Cones: Oval or round; pale yellowish brown to brown; 2 to 4 inches (5 to 10 cm) long

North American Range: Mexico and Central America

Habitat: Open woodland and forest

TREE SICKNESS

Conifers and other trees face threats from many diseases. Fungi are a common cause of sickness. Fungi may cause dead areas, called cankers, and tree wilt, or droop. Fungi may cause rust as well. Rust disease causes harmful yellow or orange spots to grow on the plant.

FOOTHILL PINE *(PINUS SABINIANA)*

The foothill pine grows throughout California in the Santa Cruz Mountains, Sierra Nevada foothills, and other coastal ranges. It has grayish-green, needle-like leaves that are about ten inches (25 cm) long. They grow in groups of three. Foothill pines may have multiple crooked trunks. The grayish-brown bark has deep splits, and it sheds to show reddish inner bark. The tree's heavy seed cones may be up to 12 inches (30 cm) long, although some are much smaller. The thick cone scales have prickles that point inward.

HOW TO SPOT

Height: 20 to 80 feet (6 to 24 m)

Leaves: Needle-like; grayish green with white lines; 8 to 12 inches (20 to 30 cm) long

Seed Cones: Egg shaped; light to dark brown; 6 to 10 inches (15 to 25 cm) long

North American Range: California

Habitat: Dry slopes and ridges of foothills and mountains

Seed cone

FOXTAIL PINE *(PINUS BALFOURIANA)*

The rare foxtail pine is native only to California. It grows as a shrub at high elevations. Its branches resemble the tails of foxes. They have very short, needle-like leaves that grow in groups of five. The two kinds of foxtail pines are southern foxtail and northern foxtail. They grow about 300 miles (480 km) apart. They have likely been separated for more than two million years. Southern foxtail grows in the Klamath Mountains. Northern foxtail grows in the Sierra Nevada. Northern foxtail has thicker bark than southern foxtail.

HOW TO SPOT

Height: 30 to 70 feet (9 to 21 m)

Leaves: Needle-like; deep green; 0.6 to 1.5 inches (1.5 to 4 cm) long

Seed Cones: Egg shaped or oval; purple to reddish brown; 2.5 to 4.5 inches (6 to 11 cm) long

North American Range: California

Habitat: Dry, rocky mountain slopes and ridges

GREAT BASIN BRISTLECONE PINE *(PINUS LONGAEVA)*

The rare Great Basin bristlecone pine can live for more than 5,000 years. It grows as a tree or shrub. It can survive cold temperatures and high winds. Its trunk is often twisted. The Great Basin bristlecone pine has thin, reddish-brown bark. It often has exposed roots and dead wood. This pine grows at elevations of 7,500 to 11,500 feet (2,290 to 3,510 m) in the mountains of California, Nevada, and Utah. At lower elevations the tree faces threats from forest fires. Its needle-like leaves may stay on the tree for more than 35 years. They grow in groups of five.

HOW TO SPOT

Height: Up to 60 feet (18 m)
Leaves: Needle-like; green with white resin spots; 1 to 1.5 inches (2.5 to 4 cm) long
Seed Cones: Egg shaped; reddish brown; 2 to 5.5 inches (5 to 14 cm) long
North American Range: California, Nevada, and Utah
Habitat: Dry, rocky mountain slopes and ridges

Seed cone

JACK PINE *(PINUS BANKSIANA)*

The jack pine grows farther north than any other pine. The jack pine may form a large, scraggly shrub that spreads across the ground or a tree with twisted branches. Dead branches may stay on the tree for several years. Its needle-like leaves are short, twisted, and stiff. They are olive green and turn yellowish green in winter. The seed cones are slightly curved. They open with the heat of forest fires and then release winged seeds.

HOW TO SPOT

Height: Up to 75 feet (23 m)

Leaves: Needle-like; olive green to yellowish green; 0.75 to 2 inches (2 to 5 cm) long

Seed Cones: Often curved; brown to gray; 1.5 to 2.5 inches (4 to 6 cm) long

North American Range: Northeastern Canada and United States, especially the Great Lakes region

Habitat: Dry, sandy, or rocky areas

FUN FACT

The jack pine is the only known nesting place for the endangered Kirtland's warbler.

Seed cones

JEFFREY PINE *(PINUS JEFFREYI)*

The Jeffrey pine grows in mountainous areas from Oregon to Baja California, Mexico. Its needle-like leaves grow in groups of three. Older trees do not have branches on the lower half. The bark smells similar to lemons, vanilla, or violets. The Jeffrey pine can be mistaken for the ponderosa pine. However, the two species' seed cones are different. The cone scales of the Jeffrey pine have a prickle that points inward in a J shape. The cones are not sharp to the touch, unlike those of the ponderosa pine.

FUN FACT

The Jeffrey pine is nicknamed gentle Jeffrey. The ponderosa pine is nicknamed prickly ponderosa.

HOW TO SPOT

Height: 80 to 140 feet (24 to 43 m)

Leaves: Needle-like; dark bluish green; 5 to 11 inches (13 to 28 cm) long

Seed Cones: Cone or egg shaped; reddish brown; 6 to 10 inches (15 to 25 cm) long

North American Range: US states of Oregon and California and Baja California, Mexico

Habitat: Moist mountain meadows and dry slopes

KNOBCONE PINE *(PINUS ATTENUATA)*

The knobcone pine grows in dry, mountainous areas. It is native to the Cascades and Sierra Nevada. It is known for its many cones. The yellowish-brown cones grow tight to the tree. They often become stuck in the growing trunk or branches. Their scales stick out and resemble knobs. They may stay closed for up to 30 years before opening with wildfire. Then the cones shed their seeds. The knobcone pine has stiff, needle-like leaves that grow in groups of three.

Seed cones

HOW TO SPOT

Height: 30 to 75 feet (9 to 23 m)

Leaves: Needle-like; yellowish green with white markings; 2.5 to 6 inches (6 to 15 cm) long

Seed Cones: Egg shaped or cylindrical; yellowish brown to light brown; 3 to 6 inches (8 to 15 cm) long

North American Range: US states of Oregon and California and Baja California, Mexico

Habitat: Dry mountain slopes and foothills

LIMBER PINE *(PINUS FLEXILIS)*

The limber pine grows from the Rocky Mountains of Canada to New Mexico. It is named for its branches. They are smooth and flexible. The limber pine usually grows as a small or medium tree. It may grow as a shrub at high elevations. A young tree's light gray bark darkens as it ages and becomes checkered with scaly ridges or plates. The tree's needle-like leaves grow in groups of five.

HOW TO SPOT

Height: 30 to 60 feet (9 to 18 m)

Leaves: Needle-like; dark bluish green; 2.5 to 3.5 inches (6 to 9 cm) long

Seed Cones: Egg shaped; light brown or yellowish brown; 3 to 6 inches (8 to 15 cm) long

North American Range: Southwestern Canada and western United States

Habitat: Mountain slopes and rocky ridges

Seed cone

PINE FAMILY

LOBLOLLY PINE *(PINUS TAEDA)*

The loblolly pine is the fastest-growing species of pine tree. The name *loblolly* is another word for mudhole or mud puddle, which references the swampy habitat of this species. The loblolly pine has a straight trunk with gray and scaly bark. The tree loses its lower branches with age. It forms a rounded shape. Its stiff, needle-like leaves grow in groups of three. The seed cones have sharp, spined scales.

FUN FACT

The loblolly pine is also called the rosemary pine for its fragrant scent.

HOW TO SPOT

Height: 60 to 150 feet (18 to 46 m)

Leaves: Needle-like; dark yellowish green; 5 to 10 inches (13 to 25 cm) long

Seed Cones: Egg shaped or cylindrical; reddish brown; 3 to 6 inches (8 to 15 cm) long

North American Range: Southeastern United States

Habitat: Hilly woodlands, moist and sandy coastal plains, and swampy areas

LODGEPOLE PINE *(PINUS CONTORTA)*

The lodgepole pine is the only conifer native to both Alaska and Mexico. It grows as a tree or a small shrub, often with a crooked shape. It can tolerate high winds and salt spray along shores. Its bark is thin, scaly, and orangish brown to reddish brown. The trunk may have large spots of resin, also called pitch. The seed cones have pointed tips, and the cones may point slightly backward on their branches. The name *lodgepole* refers to the tree's use by Shoshone groups and other peoples who used the trunks as poles for their lodge homes.

HOW TO SPOT

Height: 30 to 150 feet (9 to 46 m)

Leaves: Needle-like; yellowish green to dark green; 1.25 to 2.5 inches (3 to 6 cm) long

Seed Cones: Egg shaped; purplish green to light brown; 0.75 to 2 inches (2 to 5 cm) long

North American Range: Southern Alaska, western Canada and United States, and Baja California, Mexico

Habitat: Coastal areas, sandy or rocky areas, and mountain forests

Male cones

LONGLEAF PINE *(PINUS PALUSTRIS)*

The longleaf pine has the longest leaves of any eastern North American pine. It is one of two pine trees in the southeastern United States with long leaves. This tree's needle-like leaves are flexible. They grow in groups of three. The longleaf pine is known for its buds, which are silvery white. They grow between 3 and 15 inches (8 to 38 cm) long. The seed cones of longleaf pine trees are the largest of any eastern North American pine. Their scales have spiny tips.

Seed cone

HOW TO SPOT

Height: 60 to 120 feet (18 to 37 m)

Leaves: Needle-like; bright green with white lines; 6 to 18 inches (15 to 46 cm) long

Seed Cones: Egg shaped; deep purple to brown; 3 to 15 inches (8 to 38 cm) long

North American Range: Southeastern United States

Habitat: Coastal plains, dry areas, and sandy ridges

MONTEREY PINE *(PINUS RADIATA)*

The Monterey pine has three varieties. The most common variety grows along the California coast. The second variety grows on Mexico's Guadalupe Island. The third grows on Mexico's Cedros Island. Monterey pine bark is grayish to reddish brown with deep furrows. The tree's needle-like leaves grow in groups of three. Its seed cones may stay on the tree for 20 years or longer. They open to release their seeds when exposed to heat, such as during wildfires. This fast-growing tree lives for 80 to 90 years. Part of its scientific name, *radiata*, refers to markings on its cones.

HOW TO SPOT

Height: 50 to 115 feet (15 to 35 m)

Leaves: Needle-like; yellowish green or bright green with white lines; 3.5 to 6 inches (9 to 15 cm) long

Seed Cones: Egg shaped; yellowish brown; 3 to 6 inches (8 to 15 cm) long

North American Range: California and Mexico

Habitat: Foggy, cool, and moist areas near the sea

Male cones

PINE FAMILY

PITCH PINE *(PINUS RIGIDA)*

The pitch pine is named for its high amount of pitch. The tree has twisted, drooping branches. Its thick, reddish-brown bark is scaly and furrowed. It turns black as the tree ages. The tree's needle-like leaves are stiff and twisted. They grow in groups of three. The seed cones have a stiff, curved spine on each scale. Cones stay on the tree for several years after releasing seeds. The pitch pine is resistant to fire and injury because it can regrow from roots and stumps.

HOW TO SPOT

Height: 40 to 70 feet (12 to 21 m)

Leaves: Needle-like; yellowish green to dark green with white lines; 3 to 5 inches (8 to 13 cm) long

Seed Cones: Egg shaped; light brown; 1 to 3 inches (2.5 to 8 cm) long

North American Range: Canada and northeastern and eastern United States

Habitat: Woodlands, dry rocky soil, and near wetlands and swamps

POND PINE *(PINUS SEROTINA)*

The pond pine is found in wet areas such as swamps, bogs, and ponds. It grows best in humid habitats. The tree's needle-like leaves grow in groups of three. Its bark is brownish red with scaly plates. The pond pine grows sprouts along its crooked trunk. Its seed cones need fire or another form of heat to open. They may remain closed for up to ten years before releasing their winged seeds. The cones stay on the tree for years after opening. The pond pine can also resprout after a fire.

HOW TO SPOT

Height: 50 to 90 feet (15 to 27 m)

Leaves: Needle-like; yellowish green; 6 to 8 inches (15 to 20 cm) long

Seed Cones: Round or egg shaped; light yellowish brown; 2 to 3 inches (5 to 8 cm) long

North American Range: Eastern United States

Habitat: Coastal plains, swamps, bogs, and ponds

FUN FACT

The pond pine's scientific name, *serotina*, means "late." This comes from the long wait before its seed cones open.

PONDEROSA PINE *(PINUS PONDEROSA)*

The ponderosa pine is the most common and widely spread pine in North America. It has short, drooping branches. Older trees may have no branches for most of their height. Long, needle-like leaves grow in groups of two or three. The tree's reddish-brown bark has plates and deep furrows. Its seed cones have straight prickles and scales that curve outward. They are sharp. The Shasta people made small cakes from the tree's dried pine nuts.

HOW TO SPOT

Height: 60 to 150 feet (18 to 46 m)

Leaves: Needle-like; yellowish green with white markings; 5 to 10 inches (13 to 25 cm) long

Seed Cones: Cone or egg shaped; reddish brown to grayish brown; 2 to 6 inches (5 to 15 cm) long

North American Range: British Columbia, Canada, western United States, and northern Mexico

Habitat: Rocky hills and low mountain areas

RED PINE *(PINUS RESINOSA)*

The red pine is named for the color of its bark, which ranges from purplish red to orangish red. The bark of mature trees has scaly, flaky plates. The red pine is filled with resin. It has a strong pine scent. The tree's trunk is long and straight, but its branches may form an uneven or rounded shape. It grows a row of branches each year. Its soft, needle-like leaves grow in pairs. They snap when bent.

HOW TO SPOT

Height: 50 to 125 feet (15 to 38 m)

Leaves: Needle-like; yellowish green to dark green; 4 to 6 inches (10 to 15 cm) long

Seed Cones: Egg shaped; brown; 2 to 2.5 inches (5 to 6 cm) long

North American Range: Canada and northern United States

Habitat: Dry hilltops, slopes, cliffs, and ridges, as well as wetlands, lakeshores, and sandy areas

FUN FACT

Norway pine is a common nickname for red pine. People may have confused the tree with Norway spruce.

PINE FAMILY

ROCKY MOUNTAIN BRISTLECONE PINE *(PINUS ARISTATA)*

The Rocky Mountain bristlecone pine grows in the southern Rocky Mountains at elevations of 7,500 to 12,000 feet (2,290 to 3,660 m). At the highest, windiest places it grows low to the ground. In other areas it grows as a small, shrubby tree. It can live more than 4,000 years. Its needle-like leaves are dark green with dots of white resin. They grow in groups of five. Dead branches remain on older trees. The tree's common name refers to the bristles on each scale of the seed cones.

HOW TO SPOT

Height: 8 to 45 feet (2.4 to 14 m)

Leaves: Needle-like; dark green; 1 to 2 inches (2.5 to 5 cm) long

Seed Cones: Cylindrical to oval; dark red to purplish brown; 1.5 to 3.5 inches (4 to 9 cm) long

North American Range: Arizona, Colorado, and New Mexico

Habitat: High, windy, and dry mountainous areas

SAND PINE *(PINUS CLAUSA)*

The sand pine grows in the southeastern United States, an area that has storms such as hurricanes. The tree often leans to the side and has a crooked trunk. It may be missing chunks of its canopy. The thin, furrowed bark is gray to reddish brown. It is smoother up toward the branches. The pine's seed cones have short prickles. They usually do not open until after a fire. Sand pine trees live up to 60 years.

Seed cone

HOW TO SPOT

Height: 15 to 100 feet (5 to 30 m)

Leaves: Needle-like; yellowish green; 2 to 4 inches (5 to 10 cm) long

Seed Cones: Oval; brown; 2 to 3.5 inches (5 to 9 cm) long

North American Range: Alabama and Florida

Habitat: Coastal areas, sandy soils, scrublands, and lowlands

PINE FAMILY

SHORTLEAF PINE *(PINUS ECHINATA)*

The shortleaf pine is a hardy tree with short, spreading branches. Its needle-like, bright green leaves are flexible. They grow in groups of two or three. A mature tree's trunk has scaly, reddish-brown plates. The trunk is a yellow color underneath its bark. A shortleaf pine begins bearing seed cones at about 20 years old. These cones release seeds in fall and winter. Each scale on a cone has a short spine. The male cones are pale purple. This tree is commonly cut for lumber.

HOW TO SPOT

Height: 50 to 100 feet (15 to 30 m)

Leaves: Needle-like; bluish or grayish green to yellowish green; 3 to 5 inches (8 to 13 cm) long

Seed Cones: Egg shaped; reddish brown to gray; 1.5 to 2.5 inches (4 to 6 cm) long

North American Range: Southeastern United States

Habitat: Dry, sandy, or rocky areas, wooded areas, bluffs, and plains

Seed cone

SINGLE-LEAF PINYON

(PINUS MONOPHYLLA)

The single-leaf pinyon is a short, long-living tree. Its name comes from its needle-like leaves, which grow alone rather than in groups. They stay on the tree for 5 to 12 years. The single-leaf pinyon may have a rounded or flat shape. Its far-reaching roots help it flourish in dry conditions. It begins bearing seeds at about 35 years old. The tree's seed cones have thick scales that curve downward. Its large, heavy seeds are up to 0.75 inches (2 cm) long. Cones fall to the ground in winter or spring.

FUN FACT

Single-leaf pinyon seeds are a popular food for humans and wildlife.

HOW TO SPOT

Height: 15 to 50 feet (5 to 15 m)

Leaves: Needle-like; grayish green; 1 to 1.5 inches (2.5 to 4 cm) long

Seed Cones: Oval; green to light brown or reddish brown; about 2 inches (5 cm) long

North American Range: Southwestern United States and Baja California, Mexico

Habitat: Dry, rocky slopes and mountain ridges

SLASH PINE *(PINUS ELLIOTTII)*

The slash pine has a small range including parts of Florida, South Carolina, Georgia, Alabama, and Mississippi. Its needle-like leaves grow in groups of two or three. The slash pine loses its lower branches as it gets older. Its reddish-brown bark forms thin, shedding scales that reveal dark orange inner bark. The slash pine's wood is strong and heavy. People use it for construction.

HOW TO SPOT

Height: 60 to 100 feet (18 to 30 m)

Leaves: Needle-like; dark green; 6 to 12 inches (15 to 30 cm) long

Seed Cones: Egg shaped or cylindrical; light reddish brown; 3 to 6 inches (8 to 15 cm) long

North American Range: Southeastern United States

Habitat: Low flatwoods, near swamps, ponds, and lowlands

SOUTHWESTERN WHITE PINE

(PINUS STROBIFORMIS)

The southwestern white pine grows in the southwestern United States, including Arizona, New Mexico, Colorado, and Texas. Most of its range is in Mexico. Its soft, needle-like leaves grow in groups of five. They have fine teeth or ridges. The southwestern white pine has an uneven, open shape. Its bark is thin and rough. The large seeds from its cones are a food source for wildlife. They were also eaten by American Indian peoples of the Southwest.

HOW TO SPOT

Height: 35 to 90 feet (11 to 27 m)

Leaves: Needle-like; bluish green with white lines on inner surface; 2 to 4 inches (5 to 10 cm) long

Seed Cones: Cylindrical; light brown to yellowish brown; 3 to 10 inches (8 to 25 cm) long

North American Range: Southwestern United States and northern Mexico

Habitat: Canyons, slopes, and mountains

SPRUCE PINE *(PINUS GLABRA)*

The spruce pine grows in coastal areas from eastern Louisiana to southeastern South Carolina. A young spruce pine's bark is smooth and gray. A mature tree's bark becomes reddish brown. It forms ridges and furrows similar to the bark of a spruce. Flexible, needle-like leaves grow in pairs on the tree's branches. The trunk is often crooked and twisted. The spruce pine begins producing cones after ten years. Seed cones stay on the tree for up to four years.

HOW TO SPOT

Height: 30 to 100 feet (9 to 30 m)
Leaves: Needle-like; dark green; 2 to 4 inches (5 to 10 cm) long
Seed Cones: Egg shaped; brown; 2.5 to 5 inches (6 to 13 cm) long
North American Range: Southern United States
Habitat: Coastal plains and wetlands

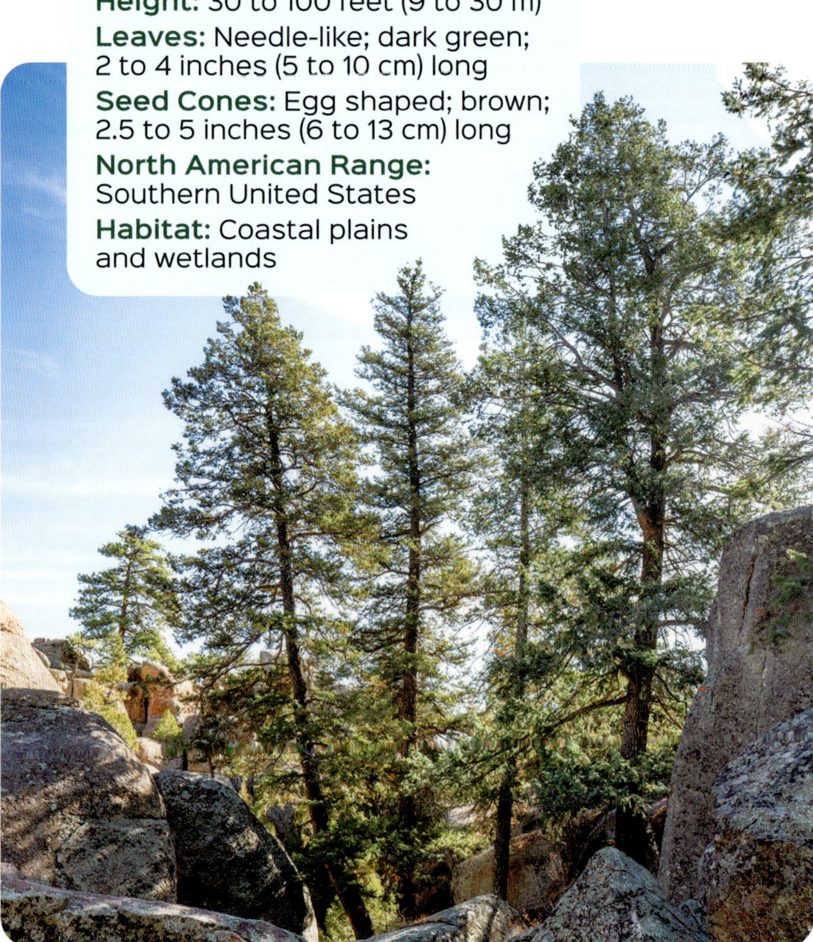

SUGAR PINE *(PINUS LAMBERTIANA)*

The sugar pine grows along the Pacific Coast. It is found at elevations of 3,000 to 6,000 feet (910 to 1,830 m). This species is known as the king of the pines. It can grow to more than 200 feet (61 m) tall. Its bark is reddish or purplish brown with scaly ridges. The needle-like leaves are twisted and stiff. They grow in groups of five. Its cones are the longest of any conifer. They can grow up to 22 inches (56 cm) long. They often weigh several pounds.

FUN FACT

The sugar pine is named for the sweet sap that comes from wounds to the tree. American Indians used the sap for food and medicine.

HOW TO SPOT

Height: 130 to 200 feet (40 to 61 m) or taller

Leaves: Needle-like; dark green with white lines; 2 to 4 inches (5 to 10 cm) long

Seed Cones: Cylindrical; brown; up to 22 inches (56 cm) long

North American Range: Pacific Coast from Oregon to Baja California, Mexico

Habitat: Coastal mountains and slopes

TABLE MOUNTAIN PINE

(PINUS PUNGENS)

The table mountain pine is found in the Appalachian Mountains. It often grows in small groups or as single scattered trees. The tree is small or medium sized. It has an uneven, rounded shape with widespread branches. Its stiff, twisted, needle-like leaves grow in groups of two or three. They stay on the tree for about three years. The bark is dark brown with small reddish scales. The trunk is about 1 to 1.5 feet (0.3 to 0.5 m) across. The tree's seed cones have a hooked spine on each scale.

HOW TO SPOT

Height: 20 to 65 feet (6 to 20 m)

Leaves: Needle-like; yellowish green with white lines; 1.5 to 2.5 inches (4 to 6 cm) long

Seed Cones: Egg shaped; light brown to reddish brown; 2.5 to 3 inches (6 to 8 cm) long

North American Range: Eastern United States

Habitat: Dry, rocky mountain slopes and peaks

FUN FACT

The table mountain pine is also called hickory pine because of its branches. They are strong and hard, similar to those of hickory trees.

TEXAS PINYON *(PINUS REMOTA)*

The Texas pinyon grows as a small tree or shrub. It is found in Texas and northern Mexico in the states of Chihuahua, Coahuila, and Nuevo León. Its needle-like leaves grow in pairs. The seeds are a food source for people and animals. They have thinner shells than those of any other pinyon. The Texas pinyon is more resistant to heat and drought than other pinyons.

HOW TO SPOT

Height: 30 to 70 feet (9 to 21 m)

Leaves: Needle-like; grayish or bluish green; 1.25 to 2 inches (3 to 5 cm) long

Seed Cones: Egg shaped; light brown; 1.5 inches (4 cm) long

North American Range: Texas and northeastern Mexico

Habitat: Dry, rocky limestone soil and dry mountain areas

TORREY PINE *(PINUS TORREYANA)*

The Torrey pine grows along the coast of southern California. It is the rarest US pine and has the smallest range of any living pine. It grows in only two natural populations. The branches form an open, spreading shape. The Torrey pine has long, needle-like leaves. They grow in groups of five. People and wildlife eat the seeds from its cones. The Torrey pine is critically endangered.

HOW TO SPOT

Height: 25 to 75 feet (8 to 23 m)

Leaves: Needle-like; grayish yellow to grayish blue green; 12 inches (30 cm) long

Seed Cones: Egg shaped; dark brown; 6 to 10 inches (15 to 25 cm) long

North American Range: San Diego County and Santa Rosa Island, California

Habitat: Dry, sandy coastal bluffs

VIRGINIA PINE *(PINUS VIRGINIANA)*

The Virginia pine grows as a small tree or shrub in the eastern United States. It is often found growing in poor soils. It has a scrubby shape, growing slowly to form a flat, horizontal top. It has short, needle-like leaves that are twisted and flexible. They grow in pairs. The tree's seed cones are small and prickly. They are sharp to the touch. The reddish-brown bark has small, thin plates. The tree's fibers are used for wood pulp.

Seed cones

HOW TO SPOT

Height: 15 to 80 feet (5 to 24 m)

Leaves: Needle-like; yellowish green to dark green; 1 to 3 inches (2.5 to 8 cm) long

Seed Cones: Cone or egg shaped; yellowish to reddish brown; 1.5 to 3 inches (4 to 8 cm) long

North American Range: Eastern United States

Habitat: Sandy soils, mountain areas, and dry forests

Male cones

WESTERN WHITE PINE

(PINUS MONTICOLA)

The western white pine grows in the northern Rocky Mountains and along the Pacific Coast. Its scientific name means “living in the mountains.” The western white pine grows quickly. It is one of the largest pine trees in the world. Its bark becomes furrowed as it ages and forms scaly plates. Its needle-like leaves grow in groups of five. Sometimes it is confused with the eastern white pine, but the western white pine’s leaves are stiffer and its cones are larger. The cones’ shape resembles that of a banana.

HOW TO SPOT

Height: 100 to 240 feet (30 to 73 m)

Leaves: Needle-like; bluish green with white lines; 2 to 4 inches (5 to 10 cm) long

Seed Cones: Cylindrical; tan to yellowish brown; 8 to 10 inches (20 to 25 cm) long

North American Range: US and Canadian Pacific Coast and Rocky Mountains

Habitat: Lowland forests and moist mountain soil

WHITEBARK PINE *(PINUS ALBICAULIS)*

The whitebark pine is a tree or shrub. At high elevations, the tree grows close to the ground. Its needle-like leaves grow in groups of five. Strong roots keep the tree sturdy even in high winds. The thin, light gray bark may be scaly on older trees. When the tree's seed cones decay, they release their seeds. The whitebark pine is known as a keystone species. That means it is very important to the survival of other wildlife in the area. The species is endangered.

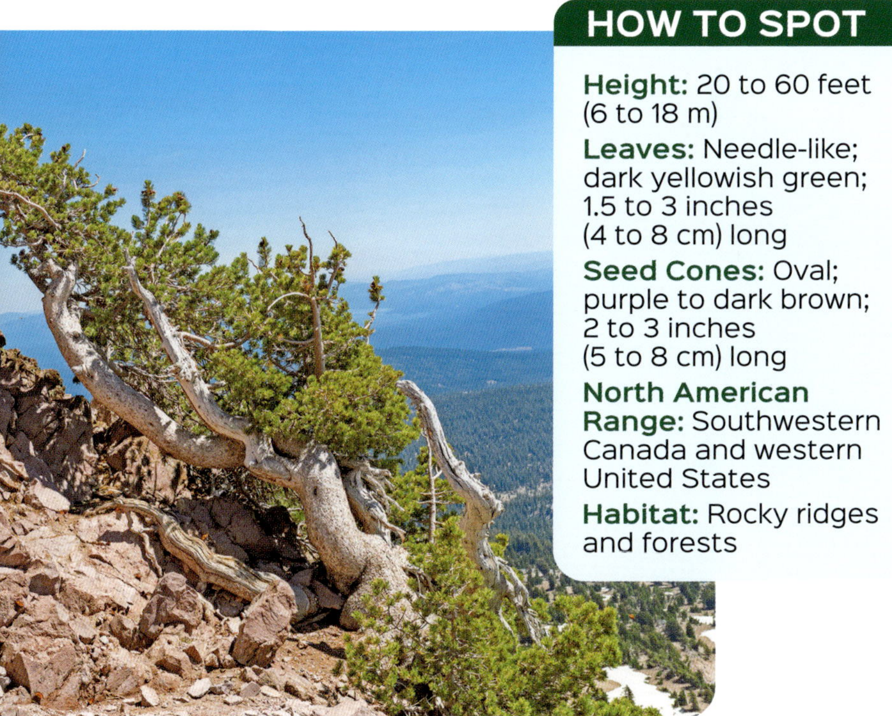

HOW TO SPOT

Height: 20 to 60 feet (6 to 18 m)

Leaves: Needle-like; dark yellowish green; 1.5 to 3 inches (4 to 8 cm) long

Seed Cones: Oval; purple to dark brown; 2 to 3 inches (5 to 8 cm) long

North American Range: Southwestern Canada and western United States

Habitat: Rocky ridges and forests

CLARK'S NUTCRACKER

Nearly all whitebark pine trees grow from seeds carried by a species of bird called Clark's nutcracker. The bird uses its beak to crack open the seed cones of different conifers. It may carry seeds up to 20 miles (32 km). It stores up to 100,000 seeds each year. The birds eat some of the seeds, and the rest grow into new trees.

REDWOOD FAMILY

COAST REDWOOD

(SEQUOIA SEMPERVIRENS)

The coast redwood grows along the Pacific Coast. It is also called the California redwood. It is the tallest tree on Earth. It grows up to three feet (1 m) each year. The California redwood is also one of the longest-lived trees. It can live for more than 2,200 years. The base of a tall tree can be more than 20 feet (6 m) across. The tree's rough, reddish-brown bark may be up to two feet (0.6 m) thick. Coast redwoods can sprout from stumps and roots. *Sequoia*, the name of this genus, was given in honor of the Cherokee chief Sequoyah.

HOW TO SPOT

Height: 60 to 380 feet (18 to 116 m)

Leaves: Needle-like; bright or dark green with two white lines on undersides; 0.5 to 1 inch (1.3 to 2.5 cm) long

Seed Cones: Egg shaped; brown; 0.5 to 1 inch (1.3 to 2.5 cm) long

North American Range: Pacific Coast of southwestern Oregon to central California

Habitat: Moist and foggy coastal plains and slopes

GETTING WATER FROM FOG

Redwoods need up to 160 gallons (606 L) of water each day. During the dry summer, redwoods rely on fog for water. They may get up to 40 percent of their water from fog each year. But climate change is a threat. As global temperatures rise, there is less coastal fog. It is harder for trees to get the water they need.

GIANT SEQUOIA

(SEQUOIADENDRON GIGANTEUM)

The giant sequoia's scientific name means "gigantic." It is the largest tree on Earth by volume. Although some trees grow taller, the giant sequoia is thicker. Its trunk can be up to about 30 feet (9 m) across and more than 94 feet (29 m) around. The tree loses its lower branches as it ages. The reddish-brown bark is spongy. The seed cones may stay closed for 20 years before opening with fire or other heat. Each cone produces about 200 seeds. The giant sequoia is an endangered species.

FUN FACT

Giant sequoia trees often live to be more than 3,000 years old.

HOW TO SPOT

Height: 250 to 275 feet (76 to 84 m) or taller

Leaves: Scale-like; bluish green; 0.1 to 0.2 inches (0.2 to 0.5 cm) long

Seed Cones: Egg shaped or oval; reddish brown; 2 to 3.5 inches (5 to 9 cm) long

North American Range: Sierra Nevada in California

Habitat: Cool, moist mountainous areas

Seed cone

BLACK SPRUCE *(PICEA MARIANA)*

The black spruce is widely spread throughout North America. Its needle-like leaves are short and pointed with four sides. They grow thinly on the branches. The leaves often appear dark when the tree stands on mountain slopes, which likely led to the common name of the species. The tree's scaly bark is gray or reddish brown. The scales of its seed cones are fan shaped. The tree's lowest branches often take root, forming a ring of small trees around a larger tree.

HOW TO SPOT

Height: 20 to 80 feet (6 to 24 m)

Leaves: Needle-like; dark bluish green; 0.25 to 0.5 inches (0.6 to 1.3 cm) long

Seed Cones: Egg shaped; purplish to reddish brown; 0.5 to 1.5 inches (1.3 to 4 cm) long

North American Range: Canada and Alaska, the Great Lakes, and the Northeast in the United States

Habitat: Swamps, bogs, and mountains

FUN FACT

Great Smoky Mountains National Park is home to protected forests made up of mainly spruce and fir trees.

BLUE SPRUCE *(PICEA PUNGENS)*

The blue spruce grows in the southern and central Rocky Mountains. It is found at elevations of 6,000 to 11,000 feet (1,830 to 3,350 m). Its needle-like leaves curve upward from the branch. New leaves are light blue. The scientific name *pungens* means "sharp-pointed," referring to the tree's stiff, spine-tipped leaves. The tree's dark gray bark is furrowed. Branches droop as the tree grows older. Seed cones hang down from the branches. They have flexible scales. The blue spruce is a common Christmas tree.

HOW TO SPOT

Height: 30 to 150 feet (9 to 46 m) or taller

Leaves: Needle-like; silvery blue to green; 0.5 to 1.25 inches (1.3 to 3 cm) long

Seed Cones: Cylindrical; light brown; 2 to 4 inches (5 to 10 cm) long

North American Range: Western United States

Habitat: Cool areas on mountains

Seed cone

ENGELMANN SPRUCE

(PICEA ENGELMANNII)

The Engelmann spruce grows in the Cascades and Rocky Mountains. It lives through long, cold, snowy winters and short, cool summers. At high elevations it grows short and shrubby. At lower elevations it grows as a tall tree. Its thin bark has loose gray or reddish-brown scales. The stiff, needle-like leaves are sharp. They grow from woody pegs on branches. The Nlaka'pamux and Secwépemc peoples of British Columbia used the bark for canoes and baskets. The roots were used to make rope.

HOW TO SPOT

Height: 60 to 100 feet (18 to 30 m)

Leaves: Needle-like; bluish green to dark green; 1 inch (2.5 cm) long

Seed Cones: Cylindrical; light brown; 1 to 2.5 inches (2.5 to 6 cm) long

North American Range: Western Canada through western United States

Habitat: High mountain slopes, stream bottoms, and valleys

RED SPRUCE *(PICEA RUBENS)*

The red spruce grows in cool, mountainous areas or other high elevations. It has a narrow cone shape. Its short, needle-like leaves are bright yellowish green with four sides. They are pressed close together. The red spruce is used to make musical instruments such as guitars, organ pipes, mandolins, and violins. Its wood is lightweight and has a light red color. Since the 1960s, red spruce populations have declined in the northeastern United States. Air pollution is an ongoing threat to the species.

HOW TO SPOT

Height: 60 to 150 feet (18 to 46 m)

Leaves: Needle-like; yellowish green with white lines or dots; about 0.5 inches (1.3 cm) long

Seed Cones: Oval; reddish brown; 1.25 to 2 inches (3 to 5 cm) long

North American Range: Eastern Canada and United States

Habitat: Cool, moist areas on mountains

Seed cones

SITKA SPRUCE *(PICEA SITCHENSIS)*

The Sitka spruce can reach heights of 230 feet (70 m). Its trunk may be nearly 23 feet (7 m) across. It grows along the Pacific Coast from northern Alaska to northern California. It is usually found within ten miles (16 km) of the ocean. Its spreading branches may touch the ground. The bark is purplish brown and forms scaly plates as it ages. Seed cones grow near the top of the tree. Sitka spruce trees have grown to be more than 1,300 years old. Insects such as the green spruce aphid and spruce beetle are threats to the species.

FUN FACT

The Sitka spruce is named after a city in Alaska.

HOW TO SPOT

Height: 40 to 230 feet (12 to 70 m)

Leaves: Needle-like; bluish green; 1 inch (2.5 cm) long

Seed Cones: Cylindrical; reddish brown; 2 to 3 inches (5 to 8 cm) long

North American Range: Northern Pacific Coast

Habitat: Cool and moist coastal areas

WHITE SPRUCE *(PICEA GLAUCA)*

The white spruce grows from Alaska to Canada and into the northern United States. It has a cone-like shape. It grows as a shrub near the tree line. Its needle-like leaves form a white, waxy coating as they age. The stiff, bluish-green needles grow on small, woody pegs. The leaves have a skunk-like scent when crushed. The gray bark has a silvery look. White spruces are used for lumber and to make instruments such as violins.

HOW TO SPOT

Height: 40 to 140 feet (12 to 43 m)

Leaves: Needle-like; bluish green with white waxy coating; 0.6 to 0.9 inches (1.5 to 2.3 cm) long

Seed Cones: Cylindrical; light brown; 1.25 to 2.5 inches (3 to 6 cm) long

North American Range: Canada and Alaska, the Great Lakes, and the Northeast in the United States

Habitat: Forests, riverbanks, and moist slopes

CALIFORNIA TORREYA

(TORREYA CALIFORNICA)

The California torreya grows in the California mountains. It is sometimes called the California nutmeg because its seeds resemble nutmeg. Male and female cones grow on separate trees. Seed cones have a fleshy covering. They ripen to a dark green or purple color. The California torreya has thin, spreading branches. Its flat, needle-like leaves are stiff and pointed. The Pomo people of California used these sharp needles for tattooing. Other American Indians used the wood to make bows.

HOW TO SPOT

Height: 15 to 80 feet (5 to 24 m)

Leaves: Needle-like; dark green; 1.25 to 2 inches (3 to 5 cm) long

Seed Cones: Egg shaped; dark green to purple; 1 to 1.6 inches (2.5 to 4 cm) long

North American Range: California

Habitat: Wooded slopes, coastal ranges, and mountain foothills

Male cones

FLORIDA TORREYA

(TORREYA TAXIFOLIA)

The Florida torreya grows mainly in Florida and Georgia. People introduced the tree in North Carolina as well. Its bark has shallow furrows and sheds in pieces. The tree has spreading branches that droop slightly. Male and female cones grow on separate trees. The seed cones resemble olives. They are purple to reddish brown. The Florida torreya is critically endangered by a fungal disease.

HOW TO SPOT

Height: 30 to 60 feet (9 to 18 m)

Leaves: Needle-like; bright green; 1 to 1.5 inches (2.5 to 4 cm) long

Cones: Olive shaped; reddish brown; 1.25 inches (3 cm) long

North American Range: Southeastern United States

Habitat: Bluffs, slopes, and wooded ravines

FUN FACT

The Florida torreya is sometimes called stinking cedar. The tree's leaves and twigs have a rotten scent when crushed.

CANADA YEW *(TAXUS CANADENSIS)*

The Canada yew grows throughout central and eastern North America. It often grows as a sprawling shrub, but it may reach five feet (1.5 m) tall and eight feet (2.4 m) wide. Stems touching the ground may take root. Male and female cones usually grow on separate trees. The female cones are red and berry-like. They are called arils. They are shaped like a cup with an opening showing the seed inside. The seeds are poisonous to people and wildlife. The tree's twigs turn reddish brown in winter.

HOW TO SPOT

Height: 1 to 5 feet (0.3 to 1.5 m)

Leaves: Needle-like; light green with 2 white lines; 0.5 to 1 inch (1.3 to 2.5 cm) long

Seed Cones: Fleshy, berry-like, and cup shaped; bright red; 0.4 inches (1 cm) wide

North American Range: Central and eastern Canada and United States

Habitat: Cool ravines, slopes, and along streams, bogs, and ponds

FLORIDA YEW *(TAXUS FLORIDANA)*

The Florida yew is a shrub or small tree with spreading branches. It grows near the Apalachicola River in the Florida Panhandle, especially on bluffs, slopes, and ravines. Its flat, needle-like leaves are flexible and soft to the touch. Young trees have purplish-brown bark. The bark becomes scaly with age. Male and female cones grow on separate trees. The female trees have berry-like seed cones called arils. The seeds and leaves are poisonous to people and wildlife. The Florida yew is an endangered species.

HOW TO SPOT

Height: 12 to 25 feet (4 to 8 m)

Leaves: Needle-like; dark green; 1 inch (2.5 cm) long

Cones: Fleshy, berry-like, and cup shaped; red; 0.5 inches (1.3 cm) wide

North American Range: Northern Florida

Habitat: Ravines, bluffs, and slopes

Seed cones

GLOSSARY

canopy
The top layer of leaves and branches on a tree.

chaparral
An area of thick shrubs and trees, often found in the southwestern United States.

endangered
In danger of extinction.

fiber
A thread-like structure in plants.

furrow
A shallow groove or trench in the bark of a tree.

genus
A group of related species of plants or animals.

hybrid
The result of cross-pollinating two different kinds of plants.

invasive
Not native to the area and causing harm to humans, animals, or plants.

mature
Fully developed and able to reproduce.

mesa
A flat-topped piece of land with steep sides.

photosynthesis
The process in which plants use sunlight to make energy, or food.

plate
A large, flat section or layer of bark.

pulp
Broken-down material used for making products such as paper.

resin
A thick, sticky material that comes from plants.

sterile
Not able to produce seeds, fruit, or other parts to grow offspring.

tap root
The main root that grows straight down; other roots grow out from it.

tree line
The line to the far north or far south that is the end of where trees can grow.

TO LEARN MORE

FURTHER READINGS

Bell, Samantha S. *Deciduous Trees*. Abdo, 2026.

Debbink, Andrea. *Trees*. Abdo, 2021.

Tordjman, Nathalie. *The Book of Amazing Trees*. Princeton Architectural, 2021.

ONLINE RESOURCES

To learn more about North American conifers, please visit **abdobooklinks.com** or scan this QR code. These links are routinely monitored and updated to provide the most current information available.

PHOTO CREDITS

Cover Photos: Shutterstock Images, front (top left, top right, upper center, middle right, bottom center), back (left); David A Litman/Shutterstock Images, front (upper left); Judith Andrews/Shutterstock Images, front (upper right); Nikki Yancey/Shutterstock Images, front (middle left); Jack N. Mohr/Shutterstock Images, front (bottom left); Peter Turner Photography/Shutterstock Images, front (bottom right); Tamara Kulikova/Shutterstock Images, back (right)
Interior Photos: Dante S. Figueroa/iNaturalist, 1 (left), 26, 47; Juan Cruzado Cortés/iNaturalist, 1 (right), 54; Shutterstock Images, 4 (top), 5 (top left), 5 (top middle), 6, 8 (top), 8 (bottom), 9 (top), 9 (bottom), 10 (bottom), 13, 14 (left), 16 (left), 17 (left), 21 (left), 21 (right), 24 (top), 25 (left), 27 (left), 27 (right), 30 (right), 31 (left), 35 (left), 36 (top), 38 (top), 38 (bottom), 39 (left), 40, 42 (bottom), 43, 45 (right), 50 (left), 53 (left), 53 (right), 58 (top), 59 (top), 59 (bottom), 60 (left), 64 (top), 64 (bottom), 65 (left), 65 (right), 67 (left), 67 (right), 68, 70 (top), 71, 72 (left), 72 (right), 75 (bottom), 76 (top), 77 (left), 77 (right), 78 (left), 79, 80, 84 (left), 85, 86, 87, 93 (top), 93 (bottom), 95, 96, 99 (left), 99 (right), 101 (left), 101 (right), 102 (right), 103, 104 (left), 104 (right), 107 (bottom), 112 (left), 112 (middle); Svetlana Mahovskaya/Shutterstock Images, 4 (bottom), 42 (top); Nikki Yancey/Shutterstock Images, 5 (top right), 63 (top), 63 (bottom), 69 (right), 73 (top), 100; Liliboas/E+/Getty Images, 5 (bottom left), 24 (bottom); Rolandas Grigaitis/Shutterstock Images, 5 (bottom right), 15; Belikova Oksana/Shutterstock Images, 6–7, 97 (left); Peter Murray/Shutterstock Images, 7, 97 (right); blickwinkel/A. Jagel/Alamy, 10 (top); Paco Moreno/Shutterstock Images, 11 (left); Sergey Denisenko/Shutterstock Images, 11 (right); William Dillingham/Shutterstock Images, 12 (top); Roger Raiche/iNaturalist, 12 (bottom); Mariusz S. Jurgielewicz/Shutterstock Images, 14 (right), 16 (right); John Rusk/Wikimedia Commons, 17 (right); Paul B. Moore/Shutterstock Images, 18; piemags/Nature/Alamy, 19 (left), 19 (right), 20 (bottom), 23 (right), 55; Mike Heine/iNaturalist, 20 (top); Phil O'Nector/Shutterstock Images, 22 (left); Mircea Costina/Shutterstock Images, 22 (right); Jeff Bisbee/iNaturalist, 23 (left); Dina Rogatnykh/Shutterstock Images, 25 (right); Wiert Nieuman/Shutterstock Images, 28; Bob Gibbons/Science

Source, 29 (left); Jon Benedictus/ Shutterstock Images, 29 (right); Stepan Popov/Shutterstock Images, 30 (left); Stuart Wilson/ Science Source, 31 (right); Puddin Tain/Flickr, 32 (top); Michael LaMonica/Shutterstock Images, 32 (bottom); Bradley D. Saum/ Shutterstock Images, 33; Martin Fowler/Shutterstock Images, 34; Erik Agar/Shutterstock Images, 35 (right); Charlotte Evelyn/Shutterstock Images, 36 (bottom); Chris M. Morris/ Flickr, 37 (left); Cathleen Wake Gorbatenko/Shutterstock Images, 37 (right); Marc Parsons/ Shutterstock Images, 39 (right); Neptalí Ramírez Marcial/ iNaturalist, 41, 46; Alejandra Peña Estrada/iNaturalist, 44 (left); Alejandro Gómez-Nísino/iNaturalist, 44 (right); John Ruberry/Shutterstock Images, 45 (left); Rick & Nora Bowers/Alamy, 48, 50 (right); Rosalina Oktavia/Shutterstock Images, 49; Francisco Blanco/ Shutterstock Images, 51; Joe Blowe/Flickr, 52, 112 (right); Al Bittler/Shutterstock Images, 56; Wikimedia Commons, 57, 62 (left), 66; Barbara Ash/Shutterstock Images, 58 (bottom); Amelia Martin/Shutterstock Images, 60 (right); Jack N. Mohr/ Shutterstock Images, 61; M. Socorro González Elizondo/ iNaturalist, 62 (right); Gary Saxe/ Shutterstock Images, 69 (left); Lukas Gojda/Shutterstock Images, 70 (bottom); Kobus Peche/Shutterstock Images, 73 (bottom); Bryan Pollard/ Shutterstock Images, 74; Ken Schulze/Shutterstock Images, 75 (top); Tamara Kulikova/ Shutterstock Images, 76 (bottom); Judith Andrews/ Shutterstock Images, 78 (right); Jason Patrick Ross/ Shutterstock Images, 81 (left); Chris Dale/Shutterstock Images, 81 (right); Peter Maerky/ Shutterstock Images, 82; Wirestock, Inc./Alamy, 83 (top); John P. Anderson/Shutterstock Images, 83 (bottom); Leigha Stahl/iNaturalist, 84 (right); H. Mark Weidman Photography/ Alamy, 88; Cristi Croitoru/ Shutterstock Images, 89; Jason Meyer/Alamy, 90; Austin R. Kelly/iNaturalist, 91; Steve Estvanik/Shutterstock Images, 92; eyeclick/imageBROKER. com GmbH & Co. KG/Alamy, 94; Irina Borsuchenko/Shutterstock Images, 98; Sandra Standbridge/ Shutterstock Images, 102 (left); Dasha Gerasimova/Shutterstock Images, 105; Irina Borsuchenko/ Shutterstock Images, 106; Matt Berger/iNaturalist, 107 (top)

ABDOBOOKS.COM
Published by Abdo Reference, a division of ABDO, PO Box 398166, Minneapolis, Minnesota 55439.

Printed in China.
052025
092025

Editor: Marley Richmond
Series Designer: Colleen McLaren
Production Designer: Ebonee Estrella

LIBRARY OF CONGRESS CONTROL NUMBER: 2024949031
PUBLISHER'S CATALOGING-IN-PUBLICATION DATA
Names: Murray, Laura K., author.
Title: Conifers / by Laura K. Murray
Description: Minneapolis, Minnesota: Abdo Reference, 2026 | Series: North American field guides | Includes online resources and index.
Identifiers: ISBN 9781098297664 (lib. bdg.) | ISBN 9798384930181 (ebook)
Subjects: LCSH: Conifers--Juvenile literature. | Trees--Juvenile literature. | Trees--North America--Juvenile literature. | Reference materials--Juvenile literature.
Classification: DDC 635.977--dc23